Quiet Healing

Quiet Healing

Teri Amar, Ph.D.

with Introduction by Lawrence LeShan, Ph.D.
author of *How to Meditate*

Northwest Publishing, Inc.
Salt Lake City, Utah

Quiet Healing

For information address: Northwest Publishing, Inc.
6906 South 300 West, Salt Lake City, Utah 84047
JAC 9.30.94
Edited by: Ann Cude

PRINTING HISTORY
First Printing 1995

ISBN: 1-56901-902-9

NPI books are published by Northwest Publishing, Incorporated,
6906 South 300 West, Salt Lake City, Utah 84047.
The name "NPI" and the "NPI" logo are trademarks belonging to
Northwest Publishing, Incorporated.

PRINTED IN THE UNITED STATES OF AMERICA.
10 9 8 7 6 5 4 3 2 1

To all those I love and learn from—
Mom, Dad, Karen, and Eric;
and to Herm—
who loves, learns, listens, and teaches—
my very best friend.

Imagine all the people, living for today.
You can say I'm a dreamer, but I'm not the only one…
—John Lennon

Table of Contents

Introduction

This book is a general introduction to the world usually referred to as New Age and to its meaning and potential for each of us. It is an excellent starting place for those of us who have wondered what all the current talk is all about: what is behind the usually vague discussions of meditation, psychic powers, mindfulness, alternate modes of reality, and the other concepts of the so-called Aquarian Revolution. It tells us what they are about and what they are good for.

Dr. Amar, out of long experience and extensive study, leads us in a readable and understandable manner, and with many illustrative examples, to a comprehension—to a level of understanding where we can decide how we feel about these matters and whether or not we wish to continue in the exploration. We learn how we personally can benefit and potentiate our own development by working with them. Her excellent bibliography tells us how to continue in deepening our understanding if we decide that this is what we wish to do.

Larry LeShan
June, 1994

I've Been There, Too!

All of my life I have been a seeker. I have looked for happiness and peace of mind everywhere. I have looked on the outside, hoping that love, money, drugs, or food could fill the emptiness that I felt inside. They never did. I have looked on the inside, hoping that psychotherapy could give me the formula for filling in the void. I found many answers, but still the black hole gaped inside of me. Along the way, I discovered that I had something to give to other seekers, if only my optimism, for I never gave up. I studied many modes of therapy (currently there are in excess of 250 therapies in practice), hoping to find answers for myself and for my patients. Some theories made more sense than others.

Cognitive psychology came close. It offers principles that can lead to an understanding of psychological functioning. Unfortunately, for me and for many of my patients, understanding how and why I thought my thoughts were not enough to dispel them. Many of my friends and colleagues found their answers in cognitive or other psychologies, but the key still eluded me.

Ericksonian hypnosis brought me even closer to finding explanations that I could apply to my own life, and a path that I could offer to my patients for discovering their own solutions. Because Milton Erickson saw people through dignified eyes, he was able to treat them with dignity and respect. Ericksonian psychotherapy has been a gift that I have treasured for myself and one that I have found very effective in working with many people. I practiced self-hypnosis about twice a week, and taught my patients to do the same. Still, my self-doubting thoughts floated, untouched, in the black space inside of me.

I am essentially an existential thinker. I believe that as humans we are capable of self-awareness—the ability that allows us to think and to make choices. This awareness endows us with freedom; we can choose the manner in which we live, and we can influence our destinies. I have always believed that our task is to create lives that have meaning and purpose. I felt excited and validated when I read Viktor Frankl's ideas in *Man's Search for Meaning*, and Rollo May's ideas in *Man's Search for Himself*. They fervently believe that we have the capacity to redesign our lives when we do this with awareness. I just was having a great deal of difficulty getting to the awareness part of the equation.

I continued my search because I knew that when I could travel through the darkness—through the dark night of my soul—I would come to a new way of being. I would touch that part of me that was my essence, and I would find meaning in my life. Even in my darkest moments I knew that if I could quiet the storms that raged inside my mind, I could discover what the purpose was of my life, and I would be able to choose to live my life in the best way for me. I had never felt as if I was able to make those choices. I was more like the reactor, or the victim of my being. Life happened and I reacted. Yet, somewhere inside, the wiser part of me knew that I could—I must—change this. If only I knew how.

Several years ago, I attended a seminar given by Joan Borysenko, a psychologist who had just written a best-selling book, *Minding the Body, Mending the Mind.*[1] Dr. Borysenko talked about her own life, the years of unhappiness and physical problems that she had endured. She could have been telling my story, for I, too, suffered not only from my thoughts, but from a variety of physical symptoms. Like Dr. Borysenko, I suffered with bronchial illness, chronic cold symptoms, spastic colon, as well as almost constant severe low back pain. When I heard her say that her savior was meditation, my interest was piqued. Among the many other forms of therapy that I had explored, I had briefly looked at meditation and rather quickly dismissed it as something that monks and hermits did on the tops of mountains.

Even with my reservations, I decided to give meditation a short trial, believing that I had little to lose. Within two weeks,

I was able to notice a change in the way I felt. Though I was still bothered by my thoughts, the intensity of my anguish was less, and I noticed longer periods of time when I simply felt at peace. After each meditation, I was left feeling younger, fresher, and more content. I had begun to travel a path that has led me to greater peace and happiness than I could ever have imagined.

There are many excellent books available today about meditation. So why write another one? Because I am certain that I am not alone. People all over the land are looking for answers, for meaning and peace and joy in their lives. Many of my patients have experienced fundamental changes in the way they experience life since beginning daily meditation. Though each of us is different, inside all of us is a core of well-being and peace. I have been changed by this process and by the work I have been doing, and I am compelled to share it with others.

May you find some of the answers that you seek in these pages. Trust that happiness and peace of mind are available to all of us, if only we look in the right places.

As Anthony de Mello says in *One Minute Wisdom*, "Nothing has changed but my attitude. Everything has changed."[2]

Chapter One
The Beginning of Change

To see the world in a grain of sand
And a heaven in a wild flower
Hold infinity in the palm of your hand
And eternity in an hour.

—William Blake,
Auguries of Innocence

The Beginning of Change

T he late 60s and the early 70s were a time for exploration. We explored the outside by landing on the moon
and the inside with marijuana and LSD. Richard
Alpert, Ph.D., was at the forefront of the research inside the
mind. He was a psychology professor at Harvard University
whose search took him from the college campus to experimen-
tation with LSD and other psychedelics, and then to the Himalayas
in India. There he discovered that meditation can be a well-
traveled path to finding the answers inside.[1] In 1971, when he
returned from India, Dr. Alpert, renamed Baba Ram Dass,
wrote *Be Here Now*.[2]

In 1971, I was a flight attendant for National Airlines,
flying all over the world, bringing a new meaning to the term
"flying high." After working a particularly stressful trip from
Miami to New York, my friend and I had relaxed in our hotel
room by smoking marijuana. We decided to spend the remainder of the afternoon wandering around the bookstore located
in the lobby of the hotel. Perhaps you have had the experience
of smoking pot and then thinking that you were really "cool"
and very intelligent. I spotted Ram Dass's book, purchased it,

and read it from cover to cover that evening. I was particularly impressed with the whole idea of "being here now." Something about the idea of living in the present touched me at the core of my being...I knew I had discovered a truth.

Today, I know that this is mindfulness, one of the primary goals of meditation. The following day my mind became the victim of the laws of state-dependent memory and learning. These laws propose that any information or behavior that is acquired in one state, as under the influence of a drug, is forgotten in the nondrugged state, but recalled again in the drugged state. This arrangement is the paradigm of "state-dependent learning."[3] In other words, the following morning I completely forgot the wonderful insight I had the previous day. In retrospect, I can see why illegal drugs are called dope.

Shortly after that experience, I left the airline industry and eventually returned to graduate school to study psychology. Though many of the learnings I had in those days were yet to become "givens" to me, one fact that remained consistent was that I was certain that the guilt, shame, anxiety, and depression that I often felt were undeniably connected to the myriad of illnesses that almost constantly troubled me. My perceived stress showed up all over my body in symptoms which included tension headaches, chronic bronchitis, pneumonia, pelvic inflammatory disease, and painful neuromas in my toe. At that time, I did not understand the mechanism that converted my emotions into my illnesses. Today we know that the immune system is enormously affected by feelings and that there are distinct psychological steps that we can take to activate our own self-healing abilities.

In 1975, Dr. Herbert Benson, also at Harvard University, wrote *The Relaxation Response.*[4] He discovered that meditation was a key toward relieving restlessness, tension, stress, fatigue, and anxiety. In addition, he reasoned that twenty minutes of meditation daily could release the body's hidden defenses against stress-related illness. Most medical textbooks attribute up to 80% of all disease to psychosomatic or stress-related origins, and Dr. Benson's findings were even more significant rungs in a ladder that was to be known later as psychoneuroimmunology. The following chapters will illustrate how meditation can be the healing bridge between the mind and the body, bringing both into more balance, and in the process bringing out and illuminating the core of peace and joy that naturally lives within each of us.

Chapter Two

Stress

We are not troubled by things,
but by the opinions which we have of things.

—Epictetus

Stress

Stress...a word we see everywhere and hear a great deal about. But what is it, why does it happen, and who does it happen to?

Stress is defined in the dictionary as "forces exerted against each other by two surfaces in contact" or "the condition of things compelling or characterized by strained effort." But stress truly means different things to different people, so it becomes difficult to define universally. The surgeon facing a long day of delicate, intricate surgery on a patient whose life rests in his or her hands may experience feelings of stress. The air traffic controller who knows that even a momentary distraction can result in a life-or-death situation for hundreds of people often experiences feelings of stress. The loan officer in a bank who is unable to concentrate because her mind is filled with negative thoughts may experience feelings of stress. A young mother becomes so angry at her five-year-old child that hitting appears to be the only solution. Undoubtedly, both mother and child feel the stress. The problems they face are different. The reactions are similar.

In the early years of the twentieth century, the chairman of the Department of Physiology of the Harvard Medical School, Dr. Walter B. Cannon, directed a series of experiments with cats. He removed the adrenal glands from some of the cats and extracted a substance from the glands. He then injected the substance into other cats. That substance has become known as epinephrine (adrenaline). Dr. Cannon noticed that all of the cats that received this substance reacted in a similar manner. Blood pressure, heart rate, and breathing rate all increased greatly. He also noted that the amount of blood flowing to the skeletal muscles rose several hundred percent. All of these reactions appeared to occur together—in other words, they were a response. Because he concluded that the animal was preparing to fight or run away, he labeled this the "fight-or-flight" response.

Some time later, Dr. Walter Hess, a Swiss physiologist discovered that stimulating a certain area of the cat's brain could bring about the same response. However, he also discovered that by stimulating a different area of the cat's brain, he could produce a very different state—one of very low energy expenditure characterized by deep rest and relaxation.

Years later, it was established that humans possess the identical fight-or-flight response. It can be brought on by injections of the same hormones that the cats received or by perceptions of stress. In humans, it was observed that this fight-or-flight response left one feeling anxious, with the associated symptoms of nausea, vomiting, diarrhea, short temper, insomnia, and headaches. As well as these not-so-pleasant symptoms, it was demonstrated that the fight-or-flight response contributed to hypertension, heart disease, cancer, back pain, and depression of the immune system.

At Harvard University in the early 1970s, Dr. Herbert Benson noticed that people who practiced transcendental meditation, a practice which involves focusing on a group of words or sounds that have a spiritual meaning (a mantra), could reach a profound state of rest and relaxation. Repeatedly focusing on the mantra had some remarkable effects—decreased breathing and heart rates, as well as less oxygen consumption. He also noticed that these physical changes were joined by changes in brain wave patterns and chemical changes in the body. He later showed that this same state could be reached via any form of mental concentration that distracted the individual from his or her usual thoughts and concerns. He called this state of deep, profound calm the "relaxation response."[1]

While the fight-or-flight response elicited various unpleasant symptoms and responses, it appeared that the relaxation response did quite the opposite. Physiologically, the relaxation response is associated with decreased metabolism, blood pressure, heart rate, and breathing rate. Psychologically, this state brings us back to desired feelings of calm, peace, and well-being that may have seemed impossible to reach.

A fascinating and intricate tapestry is this life—this body/mind being. We can see how the fabric is woven, but how can we smooth and strengthen the fibers to create more beauty, more harmony?

Assembly Line Assumptions
It has been speculated that people working on assembly

lines are susceptible to very serious stress reactions. Workers on these lines are asked to stand in one place for long periods of time doing the same thing over and over, with no creative control. They repeatedly put the same cover on the same jar or the same screw in the same hole without making any decisions or even being asked for an opinion. They are unable to make any changes—they seem almost helpless.

There are some times in each of our lives when we feel out of control, as if life were just pulling us along and we were hanging on by our fingernails. But these feelings are temporary; we are shortly back in control. It is only when we begin to be convinced that we have no control that the trouble begins.

In his compelling book *Man's Search for Meaning*, Viktor Frankl describes the grim years that he spent as a prisoner in the Nazi death camps during World War II. Besides the millions of innocent people who died in the gas ovens or were tortured and shot to death by the Nazis, hundreds of thousands of other people died of diseases like typhus that were rampant in the camps. Being a prisoner in a death camp leaves a human with very few choices of the manner in which he can live. Almost every fiber of control is wrenched from his hands, and he is left to live his life not knowing whether it will continue or will end, not knowing the degree and severity of torture, and feeling as if there is almost nothing that he can do that might change the course of his misery and despair. People such as he live lives of wakeful nightmares. They fear that:

1. Terrible things are happening and/or worse are threatened;

2. Free will does not exist. It is futile. Any hope resides in outside forces or other people;

3. There is no end in sight.[2]

I have come to believe that anyone facing a life-threatening illness is living similarly. Dr. Frankl observed that the people who tended to survive the widespread disease were those who were able to sustain a feeling of control. He learned that everything could be taken from a person but one thing: "The last human freedom—to choose one's attitude in any given set of circumstances, to choose one's own way."[3]

Feeling constantly helpless can suppress the immune system, making for more susceptibility to disease. Chronic helplessness can also deplete the brain of the chemical norepinephrine, which is vital for feelings of joy, peace, and contentment.

Not all stress can or even should be avoided. When the source of stress is clear, normal adaptive responses occur (as in swerving to avoid an automobile accident), and the mind and the body return to a level of normal functioning rather quickly. When the source of stress is chronic or ambiguous, as in the helplessness felt by prisoners of war, or if several stressors are at work at the same time, a person often does not return to normal functioning nearly so rapidly. In fact, the stress reaction continues.

Long-term stress has been clearly shown to be a major culprit in the development and progression of many, if not all, diseases. As early as 1867, physicians noted that patients who were subjected to extreme stress from extensive burns, major surgery, or other medical emergencies, developed stomach ulcers. In 1936, Hans Selye began an extensive study of the effects of stress on the body. In 1974, after many years of study, his research produced a theory of how psychological and/or physical stress is translated into psychosomatic disease by messenger molecules that travel throughout the body. He called the process the "general adaptation syndrome" and the diseases that developed as a consequence of prolonged stress, "diseases of adaptation."[4]

Later studies demonstrated that stress, whether acute or chronic, releases a whole host of hormones throughout the body. Two of these hormones—adrenaline and cortisol— have a dramatic effect on health in that they are powerful inhibitors of the immune system. When Dr. Janice Kiecolt-Glaser and her husband, Dr. Ronald Glaser, studied students at Ohio State Medical School, they showed that exam stress decreased the function of the natural killer cell. These cells are in charge of policing the body and destroying both virus-infected cells and cancer cells. They also noted that the stress of exams produced a reduction of interferon, a molecule that improves and strengthens the function of killer cells and other immune cells.[5]

All of this research shows how feelings become chemical and clearly demonstrates the body/mind connection. For instance, not everyone who is subjected to chronic stress or to perceptions of helplessness gets sick. The truth is that some people are genetically lucky—they are far more likely to stay healthy and to live longer than others. They may not be happy; they may live their lives with degrees of depression or anger or anxiety, yet they may still be physically healthy. Those others, like me, have a predisposition towards illness, and when their bodies are challenged their natural ability to fight invasion (disease) is weak, and they may become ill.

However, even those of us whose genetic makeup predisposes us to illness can find solutions and help. For me, the answer to many of my medical maladies has been meditation, which I will discuss at length in a later chapter, and exercise, which I will also discuss. For others, the answers may be different. What is common is the need to change something that we are doing. If it works, don't fix it, but if it doesn't work, don't keep repeating it.

> *Man is his own doctor and finds proper healing*
> *herbs in his own garden; the physician is in ourselves,*
> *and in our own nature are all things that we need.*
>
> —William Stoddart,
> *The Life of Paracelsus*

Chapter Three
Choices

Your mind will be like its habitual
thoughts: for the soul becomes dyed
with the color of its thoughts.

—Marcus Aurelius

Choices

The most common response to stress is to ignore it or to treat it in a reactive way (Band-Aid treatment) by finding temporary comfort in alcohol, drugs, food, and other potentially dangerous substances. All of these practices can, over time, become just one more problem from which to escape. As we have discussed earlier, left untreated, stress finds its way through the body and plays a major part in the development and/or progression of many diseases.

But what about the mind? How does stress affect the way we think, the way we feel, and the way we behave? Do our thoughts, and the importance we give to them, create a filter through which we see life?

The Worry Cycle

We all have moods, and I believe that not one of us can report that our moods are constant. They fluctuate depending on our level of consciousness at any given moment. Perhaps you have noticed that the way you see things depends, in great part, on your mood.

My husband, Herm, loves to pat me on my fanny when I

walk past him—sort of a "love-pat." When I am in a good mood, I find this habit to be very endearing and touching, and I will often stop what I am doing to smile at him. However, if I am not in a good mood, I find this very same love-pat to be annoying, offensive, and intrusive. At these times, I often have to bite my tongue to keep from telling him to keep his paws off me. Until I realized that my reactions had absolutely nothing to do with Herm, I believed that he was the culprit (or the loving man, if I was in a good mood). When I, thankfully, came to this understanding, I let him off the hook.

But what happens if we don't see the connection? What if we always take our thoughts to be real? What if you believe that what you see is real? That's when the trouble begins.

As a traveler approached the city that he was considering relocating to, he came upon an old man who sat on the side of a bluff overlooking the city in the valley below. "Tell me, old man, about this city. Is it a good place to live?" The old man replied, "Traveler, tell me of the city you have come from." The traveler answered, "The city I have come from is a terrible place. The people are dishonest and unloving. No one can be trusted, and I am grateful to have left there." The old man's response was, "I regret that you will find the city below to be much the same. Perhaps you ought to continue on your journey."

A short time later, another traveler approached the old man. "Tell me, old man, is the city below worth moving to?" Again, the old man asked, "Tell me of the city you have come from." This traveler's answer was different. "Old man, I was truly sorry to have left my old home. The people were wonderful, honest, and loving. It was a splendid place to have lived." The wise man replied, "Traveler, you are in luck. The city below is exactly as you have described. I know you will enjoy your life there."

When a person is anxious, he or she tends to try to control everything in her environment in an effort to reduce her anxiety. This produces a fight-or-flight response which, in turn, becomes a negative filter through which all perceptions become negative and pessimistic. Joan Borysenko calls the subsequent disastrous thinking "awfulizing."[1] The awfulizing thoughts create physical tension through the fight-or-flight response. The body experiences responses such as fast, shallow breathing, sweaty palms, a racing heart rate, and muscle tension in the neck, chest, and jaw. When we feel these symptoms, the interpretation is often fear and helplessness, and a perceived threat to our well being. This again activates the fight-or-flight response, which creates tension, and so the worry cycle continues.

While we are caught in the worry cycle, we activate old tapes, old tapes developed when they may have been appropriate. Later, they become conditioned, automated, habitual responses to thoughts, feelings, or situations that usually have no connection to the memory. Emotions, long ago stored in the unconscious, are brought to the surface, and we respond as we did when we first felt them.

It may well be that whatever created the belief was real: your parents were not open and loving; they were demanding and critical; you were psychologically or even physically abused. But to react to life now as if these events were continuing is useless. This is not mindfulness or "being here now." Rather, it is "being there now."

You can learn to stop these old tapes before they get out of control. To do this requires mindfulness–the ability to shift to present-tense thinking and leave the baggage of the past and fears of the future.

You will reach down into your mind to a new place of safety. You will recognize that you have reached it if you find a sense of deep peace...however briefly. Let go of all trivial things that churn and bubble on the surface of your mind, and reach down below them. There is a place in you where there is perfect peace...there is a place in you where nothing is impossible...

A Course in Miracles

Chapter Four
Listening with the Heart

If your mind is empty, it is always ready for anything; it is open to everything. In the beginner's mind there are many possibilities, in the expert's mind there are few. The beginner's mind is an open mind, an empty mind, a ready mind, and if we really listen with a beginner's mind, we might really begin to hear.

—Shunryu Suzuki,
Zen Mind, Beginner's Mind

Listening with the Heart

One of my patients told me a story that I found very interesting. It compelled me to think about how we listen to one another and how we might be able to refine our listening capabilities.

This is how she told the story:

"My husband has a habit that I find particularly annoying. Frequently, before I have the opportunity to complete a sentence, he completes it for me. Though he has known me for a very long time, and often may know how I am thinking, I feel, when he does this, that he is not listening to me, and is listening to his own thoughts. Even though I love him very much, this is one habit that I am not able to overlook. I want to know why people do this and how can they stop."

Have you had a similar experience? I have. Sometimes it is I who find myself completing someone else's thought. I know that when this happens, my mind is not quiet, and that I am listening through my programmed thoughts. At those times, my mind is analyzing everything that I hear and filtering it through my preprogrammed thoughts, through what I already know. Listening with the analytical mind is like putting a fence around our creativity—it corrals our ideas. Our imagination is then limited by what is already perceived.

Only an open mind is able to see fully. Listening with an open mind is like looking through a wide-angle lens—you can see more possibilities and have vastly more choices.

So much of our time is spent inside our mental babble. Listening through that stuff almost always brings judging, accusing, and either fitting what we hear into what we already know, or if that is not easy enough, then rejecting it.

When we are attempting to listen in this way, we are not really there. We are certainly not mindful, and all of the impressions that we come up with create the screen that filters anything else we may hear.

Only a quiet mind can touch the heart, and only by listening with the heart can we hear what is really being said, beyond the words. Whenever someone is talking to us, he or she is asking something of us. Perhaps it is only to be listened to as an acknowledgment of her worth. If this is the case, we need to respond without judgment. Perhaps she is searching for solutions. We need to be creative and open and to listen beyond the words for the feeling. It is important that we do not get on the highway of our own thoughts and mindlessly travel down an already familiar road of beliefs and attitudes.

Staying in the present, being mindful, is the key to listening. If we are listening, then listen. If we are washing dishes, then wash. If we are eating, savor the food. Don't spend the time you have wishing you were somewhere else. Whatever it is you do, do it with your heart.

Jane Nelsen, an author and a dear friend, writes that in

listening with the analyzing mind, we can often only give lip service. Listening with the heart, we can give heart service.[1]

If you don't know the kind of person I am and I don't know the kind of person you are, a pattern that others made may prevail in the world, and following the wrong God home, we may miss our star.

—William Stafford

Chapter Five

Mindfulness and Meditation

He sat still and listened to the silence. It occurred to him that for most of his life, he hadn't really listened to anyone or anything. The rustle of the wind, the patter of the rain, and the sound of water running through the brooks must have always been there, but he never actually heard them.

—Robert Fisher,
The Knight in Rusty Armour

Mindfulness and Meditation

For one who has not examined the mind and has always identified completely with passing thoughts, the possibility of being able to rest in awareness free of thought may be a bit disconcerting. It's a little like the caterpillar pointing up at a butterfly and saying, "You'll never get me up in one of those."[1]

Janice was referred to me by her gastroenterologist. Her internist had sent her to the gastroenterologist, who found no physical basis for the symptoms which almost destroyed her. Janice had begun her career as a teller in a bank almost at the same time that she and her husband, Lance, were married. At that time, Lance was well established as the vice president and heir to the presidency of a thriving food business. Just about the time that Janice was promoted to being a loan officer, Lance's business started to crumble, and his paychecks became smaller and smaller in an effort to save the faltering company. Janice was faced with greatly increased responsibility at the bank and became the main wage earner in the family. For several years Janice had exercised for at least one hour, five days a week at a local gym. However, along with added responsibility came longer working hours and less time to exercise.

Her first symptom was difficulty in falling asleep and then staying asleep through the night. She noticed that she was grouchy and oversensitive during the day. Next came the migraine headaches, and finally the stomach pains that left her doubled over and worried that she might have an ulcer or even stomach cancer. Her internist gave her pain medication for the headaches; the medicine acted on the pain but left her feeling groggy and unable to concentrate. It did nothing for her stomach pain, so she was sent to the gastroenterologist, who prescribed medicine to calm her stomach. This medication helped her stomach but did nothing for her insomnia. Frustrated, the gastroenterologist sent her to me as a last resort (which is how I get many of my patients).

Like many people, Janice came to her first appointment with all of her symptoms plus the anxiety of going to see a psychotherapist. She was nervous and certainly caught in a fight-or-flight response. When I suggested to her that practicing meditation might be a solution to some of her difficulties, she smiled the smile of a true skeptic and said something about wanting to feel better but not needing to be a better Christian. I explained that meditation might, indeed, bring her closer to a spiritual power, but for our purposes it might make her feel better physically, and would most certainly help her to feel calmer. Perhaps because of her desperation, or perhaps for some other reasons, she agreed to learn how to meditate and agreed to try it on a daily basis for a period of three weeks.

After one week, at our next meeting, Janice reported that

she was sleeping better, but that she was still taking all of the medication for her headaches and for the stomach pains. The following week, Janice had decreased the stomach medication (with her physician's approval) and appeared calmer and much happier. In the next several weeks, all of Janice's symptoms abated and she reported feeling better than she had in many years. I saw Janice for a series of twelve sessions at that time, and now, one year later, she reports that she is still meditating and that she is not troubled by any of the chronic symptoms that brought her to me.

Not all recoveries are this dramatic and not all disease originates in the mind. Too many practitioners are giving their patients the spoken or unspoken message that *all* disease is psychosomatic and that we should be able to prevent and/or cure all of our ills. If we give people that message, and they get sick or continue to be ill, we are adding to their troubles with unnecessary New Age guilt. What we have learned is that the same designs we have for changing our perceptions and for leading richer lives filled with meaning seem to lead to the fullest ability of the immune system to operate effectively. The message that we can give is that learning to be present and mindful and learning how to reach down into that core of peace and contentment that we all possess can add joy to each day, no matter what the future brings.

Motivation and Practice

A couple from the Midwest came to New York City for a visit. They bought tickets to a concert, but got lost trying to find the concert hall. Stopping a cab driver, they inquired, "How can we get to Carnegie Hall?" The cabby replied, "Practice."

Learning to meditate is much like learning to do most other things. It takes practice. But even before practice, it requires motivation and determination. The motivation requirement is often fulfilled by pain we are experiencing (physical and emotional.) If I feel bad enough, I am willing to do almost anything to feel better. The determination is something quite different.

My two favorite forms of exercise are jogging and swimming. When I first began to swim and jog, I was completely out of shape. I had stopped smoking two and a half packs of cigarettes daily only weeks before, and my cardiovascular system was still screaming for relief. My first swim was two laps in a forty-foot pool, and then I rested for the day. The following day, I jogged half a city block and rested for the remainder of the day. I was, however, determined to get into shape, so I continued to strive to do a little more each time. Now it is not such an effort to swim a mile and to jog for three or four miles. But it took, and continues to take, determination to do so.

Does one really have to fret about enlightenment?
No matter what road I travel, I'm going home.

—Shinso

Herm, my husband, began meditation about six months ago. He tells me that after just six months of meditation, his life has never been better, and that he is more peaceful and less troubled by awfulizing thoughts than he ever imagined that he would be. As an observer, I can clearly see a dramatic difference in the way he behaves. He is much nicer and less critical. His sense of humor, always good, is terrific, and he is taking better care of himself.

One morning after he had been meditating for about two months, I happened to ask him how the meditation was going for him. He answered that, although his meditations were usually good, that morning it had been a bad meditation.

Do not expect to do a meditation well. None of us learns to do it well. Anyone who claims to be able to repeat a word or a phrase for twenty minutes or longer, and not be continually interrupted by his thoughts is, I believe, either lying or has lapsed into a kind of trance. The important thing about meditation is not how well you do it, but that you do it consistently. When you are practicing, just do it! Judging how well you are doing it will take you out of the space of peace and contentment that you are seeking.

A story about Saint Theresa of Avila illustrates this point well. One of her novices remarked that it must be wonderful to be like Theresa and to not be bothered by distractions in her prayers and meditations. Saint Theresa replied, "What do you think I am, a saint?"[2]

There are many types of meditation, and I believe that they are all effective if practiced with diligence. My personal meditation, and the one that I teach to my patients, is the meditation of breath counting that is based on one used in Zen training. I have found that this meditation is easy to learn and easy to teach.

Another very popular form of meditation is one that uses a focus word, or a mantra. A mantra is a word or phrase that has a special spiritual meaning. The Eastern phrase *Hare*

Krishna or the Sanskrit *Om* are examples of mantras. Focus words can be meaningless sounds or words that may or may not have a particular personal meaning. I have worked with some people who prefer a simple word like love or peace while others have chosen a religious prayer or even a special poem.

If you choose to practice this form of meditation, it is important that you choose a mantra or focus word (or phrase) that is meaningful only to you. It can be anything at all; no one is going to judge you for your choice of word or phrase.

Should you choose to do mantra meditation, and if you have difficulty choosing your own mantra, you could try one that Joan Borysenko recommends. It is the very old Sanskrit mantra, *Ham Sah*. *Ham* means "I am" and *Sah* means "That." It is thought that the sound of this mantra mimics the sound of the inhaling and exhaling of breath. The sound of this mantra is very soothing and very easy to say.[3]

In the meditation of breath counting, as in all other meditations, the object is to be doing just one thing as fully as possible—to be mindful. Another way to say this is that meditation is training for doing only what you are doing when you are doing it. In this case, the object is to count the exhalations of your breath. I have found that it is best to count up to four and repeat. If I try to count any higher, I often get lost and forget the last number I counted. The goal is to be completely involved in the counting. Thoughts, feelings, and perceptions will intrude. Allow them to come in and to go out without inviting them in to have coffee with your soul. Thoughts are like the leaves that fall into our pool. Often, when I am gazing into the stillness of the water, a leaf will fall from a tree overhead and begin to drift across the water. I have the option of continuing to watch the water or to follow the leaf as it travels its path. It is my choice. So it is with meditation. When thoughts intrude on the counting, you can pay attention to those thoughts or you can refocus on the counting. It is your choice. Sometimes it is easier to refocus than at other times; this is fine.

As long as you eventually refocus on the counting, you are doing what you need to do. At first, I found that I was thinking and having to refocus more than I was counting. As I practiced meditation more and more, the intrusive thoughts came less often. But no matter how often your counting is interrupted and you have to refocus, just keep doing it.

It is so easy for us to judge and criticize ourselves. During the practice of meditation, it becomes easy to chastise ourselves each time our minds wander into our streams of thought. When I began to meditate, I would hear myself saying something like, "Teri, can't you do anything right?" Or, I have heard myself saying that I might just as well stop trying because there was no way that I would be able to do this. Beware of this trap. It is a trap. The mind does not want to be tamed. It is perfectly content to continue its tireless practice of awfulizing and running wildly, like an untamed horse.

It is not unlikely that you, too, may fall into this trap and your mind will try to divert you from this task, just as mine has. Be firm but gentle with yourself. Treat your wandering mind like you would a lost child. Lead it back to the path with love and compassion.

Chapter Six
Preparation and Process

If you have built castles in the air, your work need not be lost; that is where they should be. Now put the foundations under them.

—Henry David Thoreau,
A Quiet Place

Preparation and Process

It is important that you choose a quiet place, where you will not be disturbed. If you live alone, this is usually not too much of a difficulty. Turn your telephone answering machine on, or take your phone off the hook. If you have animals, like we do, they will undoubtedly want to jump onto your lap and lick you with love kisses at this particular time, so put your dogs or cats outside or in another room while you are meditating.

If you live with family or friends, ask that you not be disturbed during this time. Even small children can understand that they are not to disturb you unless the sky is really falling.

If you are used to being controlled by the wants and needs of others, this is your chance to do something for you. As soon as you begin to realize some of the positive benefits of meditation, you will be grateful that you made the effort. It is likely that others will be grateful, as well, because, if you are like many other people, meditation will allow you to be a nicer person without even trying.

Sonia came to see me when her depression had become unbearable. She reported that she felt helpless, hopeless, and angry most of the time. After three months of meditation and psychotherapy, she had changed dramatically. Among the changes, she said that she no longer felt the rage that had been a part of her for so long and which she had unleashed at everyone who crossed her path. She described the change wonderfully when she said, "It used to be that I had to make a conscious decision to be nice to someone or to act nice for a certain period of time. I could usually manage short blocks of time. Now I don't have to think about being nice. I have nice thoughts and I *am* nice."

How to Sit

Most experts agree it is important that you sit with your back straight and your arms and legs uncrossed, unless you choose to sit in a cross-legged lotus or semilotus position. Occasionally, I admit to putting my feet up on an ottoman while I meditate. I do not believe that I have negated any of the benefits by putting my feet up, and I have not found a reason documented in the literature for keeping one's feet on the ground. However, it may be important that your back be straight, as slouching can interfere with your breathing.

Some people meditate while lying down. There is nothing wrong with this position. In fact, within the last few months I have used this position, and it has been fine. I do not recommend this lying down position for anyone just beginning the practice. The mind tends to associate lying down with sleep and this can be a great excuse for it not to work—you may fall asleep. After you have been practicing meditation for a while and you have made it a part of your daily routine, you may want to try this position, or any other, for that matter. The consideration that is most important is comfort. Find a position that is comfortable for you and never mind what the "experts" promote.

The Eyes

Closing your eyes can make it much easier to concentrate, and most authorities recommend closing the eyes for meditation. There are some people who prefer to keep their eyes open and fixed on an object, like a candle, or on a spot in front of them. Herm claims that he tends to doze off if he closes his eyes and finds it easier to keep his eyes focused on a knot in the wood wall that he faces as he meditates. I believe this is a matter of personal preference, though I always close my eyes. This is another example of one reality not being any better or worse than another—just different.

Breathing

Our breath is the bridge from our body to our mind. It is the tool that can bring them together in peace and calm.[1]

Begin by taking three or four very deep *belly breaths*. Belly breaths are the ones where you fill your belly with air as you inhale, and let all the air out as you exhale. Notice how your body seems to relax as you let go of the breath. As you breathe in, your shoulders seem to rise, and the out breath is an opportunity to let them drop down and relax. After you have taken three or four deep belly breaths, begin to breathe normally. Don't try to force your breathing to be deep or to change it in any way. Just notice it and continue breathing normally. As you allow your breathing to happen automatically, you may notice that your breathing gets slower as you meditate longer.

This is due to the fact that as you relax more and more, your body requires less and less oxygen to support you.

Continuing to breathe evenly and regularly, start at the top of your head, or at the bottom of your feet, and begin to relax all of the muscles in your body. As you breathe, notice the tension that you feel in that part of your body. Let go of that tension as you exhale. Don't leave out any of the parts of you.

Begin to feel the relaxation flow through your scalp, the back of your head, your face, and your jaw. Relax your eyes and begin to feel the comfort behind your closed eyes. Using this technique, go through the rest of your body, relaxing your neck, shoulders, arms, hands, chest, back, midriff, pelvis, buttocks, thighs, calves, and feet. After you have completed this process, go back to any area that is still holding on to any tension, and allow that part to relax. This need only take a few moments to complete, but however long it takes you is perfectly fine.

The Meditation

If you choose to practice the meditation of breath counting, begin counting from one to four with each exhalation. Breathe in, breathe out, and repeat *one*. Breathe in, breathe out, and repeat *two*. Breath in, breathe out, and repeat *three*. Breathe in, breathe out, and repeat *four*. Breathe in, breathe out, and repeat *one*, and so on for about twenty minutes.

If you choose a focus word or a mantra, repeat your focus word silently in time with your breathing. Whether you repeat the word only on the out breath, or you repeat part of it as you inhale and part of it as you exhale, it is only important that the rhythm feel comfortable for you and that you continue to repeat the mantra or focus word for about twenty minutes.

Just as practice is a vital component if you wish to progress at a program of exercise or a career in fine arts, so it is an essential element of meditation. It is not so much that practice makes you any better a meditator, but that the consistent habit of meditation is what brings you the most valuable results.

To meditate once in a while, on an "as needed" basis, will have limited value. You will likely feel more calm whenever you do the meditation, as the relaxation response occurs, but the long-lasting fundamental changes that are possible with daily meditation may elude you.

> *Sometimes, I sat in my sunny doorway from sun-rise till noon, rapt in a reverie, amidst the pines and hickories and sumacs, in undisturbed solitude and stillness, while the birds sang around or flitted noise-less through the house, until by the sun falling in at my west window, or the noise of some traveler's wagon on the distant highway, I was reminded of the pass of time. I grew in those seasons like corn in the night, and they were far better than any work of the hands would have been. They were not time subtracted from my life, but so much over and above my usual allowance. I realized what the Orientals mean by contemplation and the forsaking of work.*
>
> *To some extent, and at rare intervals, even I am a Yogi.*

—Henry David Thoreau

There is no right or wrong in meditation, so don't worry about how you are doing. As soon as you start to worry, or to judge yourself, you begin to initiate the fight-or-flight response, and you start to feel anxious instead of peaceful.

Undoubtedly, you will often notice that, instead of counting your breaths, you are thinking. This is natural and happens to all of us. Don't try to not think or you may find yourself thinking about not thinking, which may lead to judging yourself for thinking, and so on, and so on. Each time that you notice yourself thinking, simply acknowledge that this has occurred and let the thought go as you refocus back to your counting. The more you fight with your thoughts to leave you alone, the more they will be with you. This is true of most struggles—the more you push for something to happen or for someone to do what you consider correct, the more resistance you get. If you let go, the struggle ceases, and you are more likely to get what you want.

Excuses

Even with these reassurances, you are likely to feel some anxiety as you begin to meditate. There are some basic reasons for this. There is an endless list of things that can distract you from your meditation. Joan Borysenko calls this the "anxiety parade."[2] You may suddenly remember that you forgot to enter a check into your check register, or a phone call that you need to make, or the lyrics to a favorite song. Perhaps the face of an old lover will pop up, along with the emotions that went with that relationship. Old hurts, new and old guilt—they all cry out for your attention. The task is to acknowledge the thoughts and feelings, and to let them drift off, as they will, unless you invite them in to analyze and agonize. Refocusing on the meditation will allow you to let those thoughts pass.

Many people get caught initially in the trap of feeling as if they are just not doing it *right*, and they can use this as an excuse not to continue. Those of us prone to perfectionism can easily say, "If I can't do it right, I won't do it at all." Don't get caught in this trap. It is perfectly natural for the mind to wander, and by constantly refocusing on the activity of the moment, counting your breaths, you are teaching your mind the art of mindfulness, the ability to "be here now."[3] This is the greatest gift you can give to yourself–the gift of awareness, of truly being fully a part of each moment that you live.

In a very real sense, the more effortful your meditation is—the more you have to refocus your mind to the business at hand—the better training it is in mindfulness. It is likely that, in time, your mind will slow down more easily and refocusing will be less troubling as thoughts become easier to let go of.

And yet, even with practice, there will be days when the conversation inside your mind is endless and refocusing is constant. As you stop judging yourself for thinking, it becomes easier and quicker to get back to breathing or to your mantra. What changes is your attitude.

Many beginning meditators report that they often fall asleep while they are meditating, so they stop meditating and settle for napping. Usually, when I ask where they are meditating, they will say that the quietest, most comfortable place is on their beds. Pavlov's dogs learned to salivate at the sound of a bell because they associated that sound with food. The mind learns by association, and it generally associates the bed with sleep. Do not meditate lying, or even sitting, on the bed.

You will probably fall asleep. Sit in a comfortable chair with your back as straight as possible. Another option is to sit on the floor in a cross-legged, or lotus, position. This began as a great position for me, until I tried to get up after twenty minutes of sitting like a pretzel. Sitting on the ground or in a chair is a matter of personal preference. As I mentioned in the previous chapter, it may be that you are able to meditate lying on the floor. Once again, the key is comfort, and there is no "right" way to do this.

When patients tell me that they have difficulty sleeping, I suggest that they do a second meditation before going to bed and that they take this time to lie down while they meditate. The combination of the relaxation response and the mind's association of beds and sleep has proven very helpful to many of them. It is very common for stress to show itself in sleep disturbances, and meditation has proven effective in many cases.

If I take a nap during the day, I usually wake up feeling worse than before, and not at all refreshed. Now, when I feel like I need some rest and I have the time to spare, I try to do an extra meditation, and I always feel recharged and refreshed after ten or twenty minutes. For me, meditation is an energy collector and serves me much better than a nap. You may find this to be true for you.

If you use meditation as a treatment for sleep problems or as an energy collector, do not substitute this for regular daily meditation. It is important that you set aside time each day for this purpose only—your time just for you.

Many people ask me if it would be helpful to meditate for longer than twenty minutes, on the theory that more is better.

My experience, as well as the reports of those who have tried it, is that the positive benefits seem to start to reverse after about twenty minutes. Many of my colleagues who practice and teach meditation report similar experiences. I have heard a verbal report of some research on this subject that is being done by Dr. Herbert Benson, but nothing has appeared in the literature at this time. I don't recommend meditating for less than twenty minutes, but it is certainly preferable to meditate for fifteen minutes rather than no minutes. If you meditate for longer than twenty minutes, good for you. Remember, this is your practice, so design it so that it suits you.

Going at it Alone or with Guidance

Often, people who know me or hear me speak about meditation ask if it is necessary to have a teacher or if one can learn how to meditate on one's own. As with most questions of importance, opinions are as varied as colors in the rainbow. Some insist that a teacher is absolutely necessary, and that without someone to watch over and to guide you, poor meditation habits may develop. Others feel differently and insist that meditation is a personal experience and that there is no such thing as poor meditation habits.

My answer to this question is not a simple one. If a person who is already having a terrific life, without undue stress, sorrow, or physical problems, wants to begin meditation as a path to increasing her joy and contentment, I believe that it is fine to read a book, such as this one, with instructions on how to meditate, and to simply begin—go for it! I can certainly promise her that she may find exactly what she is looking for.

On the other hand, many people who seek out meditation are in pain, both psychological and physical. Although I believe that meditation can certainly help them to feel better, and in time can effect dramatic changes, a combination of good psychotherapy and daily meditation may accelerate the process. As a therapist, I know that what I am doing in therapy is adding grist to the mill of my patients' unconscious minds and allowing them to find their own answers to their own questions. A question posed, a sentence heard, a word remembered, can stimulate an unconscious process that can continue later in meditation. Sometimes meditation can bring to the surface a memory, a picture, or an insight that you may want to discuss with someone in order to clarify or better understand it. A therapist is trained to help in this way.

If you believe that a professional may be able to help you to facilitate change in conjunction with meditation, be certain to choose someone who practices meditation and has felt and witnessed positive changes. If you were looking to find a foreign language teacher, it is not likely that you would choose someone proficient at grammar but with no conversational skills. Find someone who not only talks the talk, but who walks the walk.

Whether you choose to embark on your journey alone, or with the help of a qualified professional, faith is absolutely necessary. A strong belief in the positive effects of what you are doing creates an arena for change in the environment of your mind.

If you wish to know the road up the mountain, ask the man who goes back and forth on it.

—Zenrin,
The Gospel According to Zen

Chapter Seven
Taming the Tiger

The greatest discovery of any generation is that humans can alter their lives by altering their attitudes of mind.

—Albert S. Schweitzer

Taming the Tiger

The restless mind is like a boat in a storm tossed and blown about by the waves and wind. The calm mind is still and quiet, alert and aware. This is truly peace of mind.

Inside all of us is a core that is essentially peaceful and loving. This is the common thread that binds us all together, no matter the differences on the outside and the separate realities that we hold inside our heads and that shape our perceptions. Meditation has a way of touching that core and bringing it to our consciousness so that we can begin to cherish it in ourselves and to see its possibilities in others. It is nourishment for the mind and the body and, with practice, our lives can begin to have the richness of a garden of blossoming flowers.

But a garden needs attention, and if left untended, it can become overgrown with weeds that can choke and kill even the loveliest blossom. So it is with the mind. Many of us need to tend to the gardens of our minds or the weeds, planted long ago and flourishing now as attitudes and perceptions, can succeed in choking off the natural core of peace and wisdom that exists within each of us.

Arteriosclerosis occurs when plaque builds up on the inside walls of the arteries. Left untreated, the plaque can continue to accumulate and can block the flow of blood and oxygen to the heart and the brain. The terrible results can be heart attack or stroke. What happens in the mind is different but no less serious. That natural core of peace and wisdom that we are born with becomes blocked with the negative tapes that we run unconsciously through the machines of our minds.

We come into this world helpless. Though the core of wisdom and happiness is there, we are completely unable to care for ourselves and are at the mercy of those tending to our needs. It is no wonder that we develop trust and believe in those who care for us. If the messages we get are critical and unaccepting, we create guilt and shame tapes and begin to see ourselves as unlovable and unworthy. I don't believe that our parents or caregivers ever intentionally give us these damaging messages, but they see life through the filters created by the tapes that run through their minds, and if they received negative messages from their parents, then that is how they see life.

I am an only child and very much loved and cherished by my family. I am certain that my parents wanted only for me to be happy and to be the best possible me, yet their way of accomplishing this had a reverse affect that plagued me for many years. Whenever I accomplished anything, whether it was a good grade or a part in the school play, they would first praise me and then compare me to a cousin or to the child of a friend who had done even better. They would always say things like, "Teri, you're smarter (or more talented, or prettier) than so-and-so, and we know you can do at least as well as she did." Whatever their words were, the message I received was that nothing that I did was of any value or was good enough. I carried that tape around with me for many years, playing it over and over again until I was convinced that I really couldn't do anything right. When I did manage to accomplish something, I made sure to compare myself to someone who had accomplished more, thus negating the self-affirming value of accomplishment. If I was praised by someone else, I waited for the ax of comparison to fall. If that didn't happen, I put my own words to the music of praise and thought things like, "If they knew the real me, they wouldn't be praising me."

A child who believes that nothing she does is good enough does one of two things, or both. Either she keeps trying to accomplish things that will bring the long-sought approval from Mommy and Daddy, or she gives up trying to accomplish anything at all. I managed to do both. When all of my efforts failed to bring me the approval that I believed I needed to be whole, I simply gave up. For some time, I stopped trying. It was not until I began to heal that wounded little girl that I was truly able to feel self-worth and self-efficacy, and to believe in myself. Meditation was the most effective tool for me to begin the healing process.

Most of the people I see today in my private practice are facing life-threatening illnesses: cancer, AIDS, coronary artery disease, ALS (Lou Gehrig's disease). The more people I work with, the more of a pattern I have begun to see, both among people facing physical illness and pain and among people who are feeling deep, scalding emotional pain. Almost without exception, people who found their way into my office were living in a land of lost or unrecognized dreams, or they were living someone else's dreams.

I began to look at how this can happen. How can so many of us live lives of pretense and emptiness? If you look at children, you notice that they come into the world with all the self-confidence they need. They are open and creative and they are natural healers. But often children are not nurtured. Worse, they are encouraged or forced to fit into someone else's mold. They are too often told that there are particular "right" ways to be and particular "right" paths to follow.

The implicit message that children understand is that unless they live within the parameters of what is "right," they are not good enough. In fact, they begin to see themselves as bad, or "wrong."

When this happens—when a unique, one-of-a-kind human being tries to live someone else's dream, the spirit begins to die. As a person becomes spiritually crippled, the crippling extends to their bodies.

If a person such as this is never challenged by illness, he may go through life living in someone else's dream, and he may only recognize and acknowledge this truth in the silence of the night or in the low level of depression he lives with.

If he is challenged—if his body is challenged, his natural ability to fight invasion (disease) is weak, and he may become ill.

Therefore, we must attend to this inner child, this little person that lives inside all of us, and we must let those children (and ourselves) know that there are choices for them, for all of us. We must recognize that healing toward wholeness takes work, and that we must change. I believe that the whole idea of being resistant to change is that we are afraid that as we change we will lose something we need. We must teach ourselves that change is an opportunity to move and to grow— to go in the direction of wholeness.

I am not certain precisely how meditation helps to accomplish this miracle of change. I have heard many theories and have some of my own. Perhaps, by training the mind to be present, to be mindful, we begin to develop a sense of control. While we are meditating, we are constantly having to refocus our minds, to go from thinking our thoughts to concentrating on our breathing or on our mantra. I believe that this training can generate a sense of self-control and personal power that can have far-reaching results.

I also believe that meditation allows the unconscious mind to return to the impasse, to the place and time when we created the belief through which we are now seeing, and to redo that event so that a different, healthier perception develops. Researchers such as Pelletier[1,2] and Kornfield[3] have reported that meditation increases adaptive regression. I believe that this happens at an unconscious level so that we are not even consciously aware that the healing work is occurring. What we are aware of is a change in attitude and perception. At some point in my own meditation, I just began to feel better about myself. I began to trust myself more and to value myself. But the changes were, and continue to be, subtle. It's a gradual shift from seeing the glass as half-empty to seeing it as half-full.

Mindfulness—Freedom to be Here Now

The Japanese have for centuries known and taught about mindfulness. They are also famous for their gracefulness and attention to detail. I believe that the method they use to teach their young to serve tea is a wonderful illustration of mindfulness. When Japanese children are taught to serve tea, no tea is used. The children learn to serve tea without having to concern themselves with the liquid spilling or scalding them. All of their attention can focus on the service itself.

There have been times in all of our lives when we have experienced mindfulness. Perhaps you have been listening to a piece of music that you particularly enjoy. Time and thought seem to vanish, and all that matters is the music and your response to it. Possibly you have started to read a book that you find compelling and captivating. All of a sudden you glance at your watch and notice that an hour has just flown by. At times such as these there is no past and there is no future—only the present, with all of its texture and richness.

Several years ago, I went to northern California to study hypnosis with Deborah Ross, Ph.D. Deborah lives and teaches on a wonderful ranch that sits on the top of a mountain in Los Gatos. She has done a tremendous amount of work to create an environment that is peaceful and conducive to growth and learning. One of the things she has done is to build a wooden deck outside her kitchen and dining room. She has installed a hot tub on the deck, and the view of the valley below is breathtaking. Professionals who come to study with Deborah live with her at the ranch for several weeks and are all given chores to do around the house.

My chore, on a particularly beautiful afternoon, was to wash the dishes that could not be put into the dishwasher. My colleagues had decided to spend the time after lunch frolicking in the spa. I stood at the sink, looking out the window at my friends relaxing and laughing in the spa while I washed dishes. Within a very short time all of my old "poor me" tapes started running. Then came the "why me" tapes, which led to the anger tapes, which soon led to my dropping and breaking one of Deborah's favorite platters. Of course, I immediately felt shame and guilt, those familiar emotions that always follow my old negative tapes. Though I wished that I could have stuffed myself into the drain and turned on the disposal, I told Deborah what had happened. Her response was one that touched the truth in me and has stayed with me since. She calmly said, "Teri, if you had been more mindful, you might have enjoyed the feeling of the soap and warm water touching your hands, and you may have appreciated the feeling of the smooth surface of the dishes as your fingers touched them. Instead, you were someplace else completely. There is a lesson in this for you."

Indeed, there was a lesson for me and for many of us. Mindfulness is common everyday meditation. It is allowing life to happen without the confines that we construct by looking through filters created long ago. It is an openness to the moment and all that each moment engenders. Each moment is unique, unlike any other, and dictates that we pay attention to not only what is happening on the outside, but to our thoughts and feelings. Not all moments are pleasant, and bad things do sometimes happen, but if we are to grow, we must learn from the process of living, and not from our reactions to life.

Being present is not knowing about something. It is knowing the real essence of that thing. I love to jog, and often, during a really good run, the only awareness I have is the movement of my body, the feelings in my feet as they touch the ground, and the particular rhythm that I have achieved on that run. I am unaware of time, both past and future, or of the scenery around me. It is as if I am not only the runner, but also the run itself.

The ability to be mindful is what I believe separates the artist from the craftsman. My husband, Herm, and I love the ballet and go to many of the performances of our city's ballet company. In a recent performance, I was able to see the difference between artist and craftsman. In one ballet, it was clear that all of the dancers knew their steps and all the moves, but there was no feeling, no soul to the performance. The next ballet, a *pas de deux*, was quite a different experience. It was as if the dancers were not playing parts in a story—they were the story and they were their characters. It was beautiful and a privilege to watch their performance. This is mindfulness— the difference between knowing *about* something and know- ing something itself.

> *[A] joy will open our hearts like a flower, enabling us to enter the world of reality.*
>
> —Thich Nhat Hanh,
> *The Miracle of Mindfulness*

Chapter Eight
The Tricks of Mindlessness

"Why is everyone here so happy except me?"

"Because they have learned to see goodness and beauty everywhere," said the Master.

"Why don't I see goodness and beauty everywhere?"

"Because you cannot see outside of you what you fail to see inside."

—Anthony deMello,
One Minute Wisdom

The Tricks of Mindlessness

It is almost always the filters through which we see the world, at any given moment, that determine our reality. The filters were created as part of our system of rules and principles that, early on, helped us in our childlike attempts to understand the world. Along with our need to understand the world, we also did whatever was necessary to attempt to insure our safety. The safety was not so much an external one, though we learned not to touch the hot stove, as it was an internal safety that kept at bay our fears of rejection and abandonment. Though often these rules and laws went against the natural wisdom with which we were born, it was the only way that we knew to feel safe.

Still, we tend to cling to these rules, and the filters we construct from them, in a less than mindful manner. We mindlessly assume that what we are seeing is real, instead of recognizing it as an interpretation that is colored by a filter created long ago.

Sweeping generalizations are mindless. "Jews are cheap, Blacks are lazy, Irish are drunks, Orientals are hard workers, French people are arrogant and do not like Americans, men are insensitive, women are too sensitive…" The list could go on and on. How do we get these ideas? Usually, they are passed on from generation to generation.

Craig was a fifteen-year-old who had been referred to me by his high-school advisor. Craig was an exceptionally bright young man from a family that had lived in South Florida for several generations. His father was a prominent attorney and his mother was active in several charities. Craig had done well at the private schools he had attended, both socially and academically. When finances necessitated that Craig return to public school, he began to have some trouble. At first, he got into minor scrapes with certain of his classmates. Soon, he joined a gang and was constantly in trouble at school. His grades dropped, and he began to skip school regularly. Soon Craig was buying, using, and selling crack cocaine.

What made the greatest impression on me about Craig during our first interview was his extreme hatred for anyone different from him. He made Archie Bunker seem like a liberal! It occurred to me that a young man would have to have been exposed to a lot of hatred to be so rooted in bigotry. I decided that family therapy was in order, and I was not at all surprised when at our first meeting Craig's father was very interested in my ethnic background. His bigotry was not as blatant, but just as treacherous.

As a family therapist, I am frequently reminded that children will mirror their parents, both in the actions they take and in the beliefs they hold.

The mindless beliefs that we continue to accept as truths create the reality that we live in. Those filters don't always come from our parents. We do quite a job of creating our own truths. Usually, what we believe turns out to be a self-fulfilling prophecy. I come from a family that used food as a reward and a pacifier, and all through my childhood and adolescence, keeping my weight down was a battle. Adolescence is enough of a struggle, and the added burden of feeling fat was tough. I was convinced that I was unattractive and that boys did not like me.

I was a member of a youth group sponsored by the synagogue that my family belonged to, and each month the youth group held a dance. I would get all dressed up for the dance only to spend much of my time talking to the other girls. Those dances convinced me that I was correct—I was fat and ugly and totally unattractive.

A few years ago, I went back to the town I grew up in for a twenty-year high school reunion. At the cocktail party on the first night of the reunion weekend, a man asked me to dance. This man, Bob, was the very same Bobby who had not given me the time of day when I was thirteen. My first response to Bob was, "So, where were you when I needed you?" His answer left me reeling. He said, "Teri, you were such a snob and so aloof that we were all afraid to talk to you."

We create our own mind truths, and then we become the prisoners of our minds. I went through some terribly painful times based on my mindless assumption that someone else's behavior was evidence of my truth. Mindless assumptions can, and do, create realities.

A few years ago, Herm and I went to France. Our experience of French people was very different from that of many others. We found these people to be friendly, helpful, and charming. One evening Herm and I were enjoying dinner at a bistro mostly frequented by local French people. A group of four people came in and asked to be seated. I knew they were Americans from their speech. When the hostess told them, in broken English, that there would be a brief wait for a table, the Americans started to pout. They all got disgusted looks on their faces and began complaining to one another. The hostess tried to remain cool, but soon she, too, had an attitude problem and acted aloof to the Americans. Soon, everyone was angry at everyone, and relations between America and France took a hit.

Mindlessness and the ego walk hand in hand. The ego wants to find reasons for everything. If we feel good, the ego wants to explain why and take the credit. If we feel unhappy, the ego connects our pain to something bad. It goes quickly to our warehouses of negative emotions and bad opinions that we have accumulated over the years and diligently saved for times like these. Without stopping to examine the new situation, it jumps quickly to pull out of the bag an old perception that can fit this situation, and we are again the prisoners of our minds. How different our days might be if we stopped to become aware of each situation. We would be free to choose our reactions and to learn something new. Prisoners have few choices.

All of our wired-in network of thoughts have been with us for all time. They are familiar. Though often sad, it's all we know. Therefore, we assume that these thoughts are real—they are our realities. Meditation loosens this wiring, lets in the fresh air and sunlight, and allows for moments of clarity.

Meditation frees us to put our awareness where *we* decide to, instead of being grabbed, shoved, or pulled along by our thoughts.

"It's as if you lived in a little town and you go up to a mountain top and, looking down, you see how you move about in the course of an ordinary day. You see your route to work, how you go shopping, the main thoroughfares, your shortcuts, your daily routines—you're seeing all that from up there. Then you return to the village. But now, when you're moving around town thereafter, there's a part of you still watching it all from up there."[1]

When we are functioning from the cores of wisdom and peace that exist within all of us, rather than from those parts of us that analyze and examine (our thought system), the results can be wondrous. Often, we can find solutions to problems without the effort of figuring them out. It's as if all the answers lie dormant inside of us and are able to automatically be called up, as in retrieving a file from a computer directory.

Natural optimism and natural positive thinking are all available. We can look forward to increased openness, faith, resiliency, spontaneity, love, compassion, and a desire for pleasure. As we unclog the channel of wisdom, we may be more open and alert to opportunity and more likely to attempt something that may have seemed impossible before (like writing this book was for me). Not only might we be more likely to attempt the previously unattainable goal, but we are more likely to keep at it, and to not give up when the going gets rough.

Susan was a compulsive shopper. The bumper sticker saying, "When the going gets tough, the tough go shopping," seemed created with her in mind. She came to therapy after her landlord had threatened to evict her for nonpayment of rent for several months and three banks were threatening court action for not paying her credit card bills, which had been taken to the limits of available credit. She owed over $37,000, and anxiety had become as familiar to her as breathing. She was unable to sleep and was losing weight at an alarming rate. During our first meeting, she was able to say that the only way she had ever been able to deal with stress was to "treat herself to something nice." I wondered, aloud, how her parents had coped with stress, and her answer was not at all surprising. She said that her dad had extramarital affairs and her mom was an alcoholic. Certainly, her modeling had been poor, and adaptive coping skills were not something that she was taught.

My first intervention was to send her to a qualified credit counselor to deal with the monstrous bills she had accumulated. On a deeper psychological level I encouraged her to begin meditation and therapy to learn about stress, thought, and perception. I felt certain that meditation would help her to begin to feel a sense of control and power in her life, and in conjunction with psychotherapy, could significantly help her.

She was impatient, as are most people who are in pain. She reported, after two weeks, that the treatment was a failure. She could not meditate "right" and was certain that medication, and not meditation, was the answer for her. Sometimes, I do feel that medication can be used effectively with therapy, but not in Susan's case. I encouraged her to continue meditating and coming to therapy, perhaps using blind faith.

Susan stayed in treatment for three months until the

company she worked for transferred her. She had made many changes, and was much happier, though not where she wanted to be. I recently received a note from her, ten months after she moved. She wrote that she was still working with the credit counselor, and was paying off her debts. She no longer used any credit cards, and she wrote, "Though I may get anxious, I regain my peace more rapidly. Sometimes I get angry, but I let go of the anger more quickly. I am less and less consumed with the guilt that I always felt when I became angry. More and more, I am simply aware when those feelings arise and I do not judge myself for feeling them. It seems as if not judging myself allows the feelings to pass quickly, without my hanging on to them."

I believe that meditation helps us to grow more comfortable with ourselves as beings in the universe. As this takes place, we are introduced, or reintroduced, to parts of ourselves that are long lost or forgotten. We begin to understand that we are not alone, and that where we are, wherever it is, is all right. We come to know that "Out of this world we cannot fall."[2] The knowledge and understanding of our unique separateness is enhanced by knowing how connected we all are.

As meditation deepens, compulsions, cravings and fits of emotion begin to lose their power to dictate our behavior. We see clearly that choices are possible: we can say yes or we can say no. It is profoundly liberating.
                                                    —Eknath Easwaren

Chapter Nine

More Potholes to Watch Out For

The result is not the point; it is the effort to improve ourselves that is valuable. There is no end to this practice.

—Shunryu Suziki,
Zen Mind, Beginner's Mind

More Potholes to Watch Out For

David and Laura had been married for several years. Each week, they tried to make the time to go out on a date with each other. At other times, they went out with friends or took the kids along with them, but they attempted to spend time only with each other at least once a week. On a particular evening, they decided to go out to dinner and then to a movie. They happened to order the same food for dinner, and as they left the movie theater, Laura turned to David and said, "This has been a wonderful evening. Dinner was delicious and the movie was terrific." Surprised, David turned to her and said, "I hated the food and the movie was a total bore."

Perhaps you can imagine what followed. Laura tried to persuade David that the food had been great, and to convince him of the fabulous acting and storyline of the movie. David held his ground, and soon they were slinging mud at one another. Laura accused David of an inability to like anything, while David stated that Laura liked everything because she had no taste.

Is it possible that they were both right? Was the movie both bad and good? Was the food delicious as well as awful?

I believe that before we learn to read and write, we should learn the principle of separate realities. It is a fundamental concept that seems to elude most of us.

Sue Pettit, a gentle woman and poet, illustrates the concept wonderfully in "Green, Not Blue," from *Coming Home*.

I was out for a walk
when I happened to meet
the woman next door.
She was new on our street.
She nodded her head,
I returned her a smile.
And I thought
She seems nice.
We've a similar style.

The next day we met,
I took over some flowers.
We hit it off well.
We talked several hours.
She told me of her life.
I told her of mine.
And I thought
I do like her.
This new neighbor's fine.

Then one day in the yard,
it is shocking but true,
this new friend of mine

called my green grass blue.
She kept calling green blue
'til I got so upset.
And I thought
I don't like her.
I'm sorry we met.

In everything else
we had seen eye to eye;
from the red of the rose
to the blue of the sky.
Now she disagreed firmly
with no hesitation.
And I thought,
I am right,
and I'll get validation!

I called over Marie,
a real long time friend.
I just had to give
this discussion an end.
"Marie," I said, "Tell her
that this grass is green!"
And I thought
What a neighbor
to make such a scene.
Marie looked at it closely,
examined it's hue.

She saw lots of my green
not a hint of her blue.
So I nodded my head
and I folded my arms.
And I thought
Whew, I'm right.
There's no cause for alarm

But my neighbor just smiled
and she said, "It's okay.
I just happen to see
your green grass my own way."
She wouldn't admit
that she saw green all wrong.
So I thought
With her outlook
our friend days are gone.
So I stopped going over
to visit with her.
What I saw and she saw
just didn't concur.
We couldn't be friends
'cause we didn't agree.
For I thought
All my friends
have to see just like me.

As the years passed me by
lots of friends passed by too.

Over matters important
like green versus blue.

Just one little difference
could lead to a fight.
'Cause I thought
In my world,
there is only one right.

I'm much wiser now.
I don't see the same way.
My heart
not my eyes
looks upon each new day.

When I look from my heart,
friends are blessings to me.
Without thought
There is room for all colors,
I see.

Separate realities are evident everywhere. Rarely do two people, let alone two countries, see the world in exactly the same way. Each one of us has a set of unique filters through which we see, depending on our mood. These filters are made up of beliefs passed on to us by others, memories and feelings stored long ago that comprise our thought systems. The messages that I got from my parents were likely different from those that you received, and though in many important ways we may see life similarly, I am certain that in lots of ways we see differently.

I throw out my garbage. Herm "pitches" it out. Herm loves opera, while I compare most opera to the sound a fingernail makes when scratched on a blackboard. The word is out that George Bush prohibited broccoli from being served at the White House. I eat broccoli, and love it, at least five times a week. Am I going to say he is wrong for not liking broccoli?

Our perceptions are not wrong or right. They just are. But if I am convinced that it has to be one way or the other—either you're right or I am—than we will eventually have a problem. I am either going to try very hard to convince you that I am right, or I am going to live with feelings of inadequacy and insecurity. Neither space feels good for very long and both can lead to feelings of loneliness and isolation. If the primary filter through which I see has written in bold print MY WAY OR THE HIGHWAY, and that is how I see life, I am naturally going to do a great deal of judging. Judging takes away peace faster than you can imagine.

Suppose you are driving down the road and another driver cuts in front of you, causing you to swerve to avoid an accident. Do you swear at him or her, or do you think *very* unkind thoughts about that person? Imagine the scenario for a moment…How do you feel? Tense? Anxious? Where is your peace of mind? It got lost in your judgment. Judgment robs us of our wisdom and our ability to see clearly. Perhaps that other driver was ill, or rushing to reach a sick relative. Whatever the reason, is it worth losing your peace of mind over?

If my self-esteem is in direct proportion to my being right,

I have to convince you to see things my way and I am compelled to judge you if you don't.

Meditation allows you to begin to value yourself without judgment. As you begin more and more to see yourself as acceptable, you will be able to see the beauty and value in others. Judgment can become observation, and peace of mind can become the natural state of being.

Can this miracle happen overnight? I believe that almost anything is possible, but it is far more likely that this, like any change, will be a process that happens over time. When you begin to make soup, you put all of the ingredients into the pot and stir. If you taste what you have at that point, you will not get the same flavor as you will if you wait until the ingredients have blended and simmered. If you take small tastes along the way you may notice small changes in the tenor of the mixture, but the real essence of the soup will emerge later on, at the proper time.

I enjoy making split pea soup. I start with hard dried peas that taste something like rocks, water, and a great deal of herbs and spices. When I first put them in the pot, the mixture tastes like water with rocks. After about one half hour, the taste is like flavored water, with rocks. Should I give up on my effort at that point, because it doesn't yet taste like rich, creamy split pea soup? Perhaps, but what a waste. Meditation is similar. It takes time for the mind to simmer and to find the natural flavor of joy mixed with meaning and peace. One of the most precious effects of meditation is how it restores our ability to recognize, value, and nurture our childlike qualities, our capacity to trust and rejoice in wonderment.

This morning I went out for a leisurely jog through my neighborhood. As I ambled along a path that winds through a nearby park, I observed a group of children who embody the essence of what we can hope for, what naturally exists within all of us. The children, a group of about twenty, were of all colors and sizes: black, white, red, yellow, fat, skinny, tall, and short. There they were...on this beautiful day, in a field of green. They were holding hands and dancing in a circle...all smiling and singing songs of joy. I know that same joy is available to all of us. We only have to look.

Chapter Ten
Beware of Definitions

We are never only one way. Like the seasons, we change and, like time, we evolve.

—Teri Amar

Beware of Definitions

Beware of defining yourself, or others, too narrowly. If you think of yourself primarily as one way, you may be denying all the rest of the resources that are available to you as a human being.

It is so easy for us to make a sweeping generalization whenever we are unable to explain away a problem or to find a reasonable interpretation for our, or others', actions.

Sarah never went to college. She grew up in the Midwest in a family that placed a great value on working. The unspoken rule was, Experience is the best teacher. Sarah worked at a part-time job all through high school, and as soon as graduation was over, she went to work full-time in the family business. For many years, the family had owned and operated a series of bars and cocktail lounges. Sarah learned early on how to mix and serve drinks, as well as the art of managing people. The family lost the bars after a key employee embezzled a great deal of money and the bank foreclosed on their mortgages. Sarah moved to Miami, where she met and married Tim. Tim was an accountant who had graduated from college with high honors. Whenever Sarah and Tim argued,

Tim ended the discussion by saying things like, "Don't argue with me. You never went to college and you don't know anything about this." His other favorite observation was, "That's a really stupid thing to say." If he became really excited, he might even say, "You are truly stupid."

Sarah and Tim had been married for nine years when Sarah came to counseling. She had been referred by her physician, who had diagnosed her hypertension as stress-induced. Sarah learned to meditate and began seeing me for psychotherapy. I suggested that Tim and she begin couples therapy, but Tim refused, claiming that the "problem" was not his. All efforts to bring Tim in for therapy failed. Sarah soon made some significant discoveries about herself. Perhaps the greatest understanding that she had was that she believed she was truly stupid. So many years of giving herself that message, combined with the messages from Tim, had convinced her of that. After some months of psychotherapy, and daily meditation, Sarah made some decisions. Not surprisingly, she decided to leave Tim.

The other decision she made was to go to college. She enrolled as a day student so that she could work as a bartender at night to support herself. Sarah phoned me last week to tell me that she had made the dean's list this semester.

We are never only one way. Like the seasons, we change and, like time, we evolve. Assuming we are always the same is a belief that is terribly limiting. We are not exclusive about creating negative beliefs. We don't just create them about ourselves. We create broad, expansive beliefs about other people, about the past, and even about the future.

My friend Diane phoned me today to share an important insight she had just had. Diane is the oldest of three sisters. For as long as I have known Diane, she has believed that her parents did not love her as deeply as they had loved her sisters. She claimed that her sisters were held and hugged often, while she was rarely touched. Diane claims that her relationship with her father was a positive one (he passed away several years ago), but her connection with her mom has always been strained and riddled with resentment. This morning she spent a few hours looking through old family albums. What she saw this time astonished her. She told me that she saw, in every photograph of her mother and her, love on her mom's face. She saw her mother holding her, laughing, and kissing her, and being happy with her. Though Diane's mother is a lovely woman, Diane has often said that she believes her mom is unattractive and very "hard" looking. Today, her mother looked "beautiful...a real knockout." Perhaps the most astounding discovery Diane had today was in what she saw when she looked at a family portrait taken at her youngest sister's wedding. She said that almost everyone in the picture was smiling and holding hands. She alone had her arms crossed in front of herself as if wearing an imaginary straitjacket. Today Diane said, "I wasn't the victim. They were victims, and now I can begin to forgive myself."

Diane's family didn't change. They did not suddenly become loving and affectionate. Her eyes changed, so how she saw her past was altered. What you see is what you get. If you see your life in one way, that is how it will be. If you see yourself in a particular way, that is how you will be.

It is very easy to create a limited future. All I have to say to myself is, "All lawyers are thieves," and I'll be certain to have a negative experience the next time I meet with an attorney. Whatever my thought is, good or bad, reality is sure to validate it. If I think all attorneys are larcenous, I will act suspicious and untrusting, perhaps creating a suspicion that I am withholding something, or that I have something to hide. I certainly will not encourage on open, trusting relationship with mutual respect. How is an attorney going to react to my suspiciousness? Possibly by wanting nothing to do with me, and by withdrawing from my case. How will I interpret that? "That so-and-so took my deposit and then abandoned me. I was right. All of them are crooks."

Thoughts are the connecting elements in a feedback loop of life. I can create a pleasant reality based on my thoughts just as easily.

Mickey believes that human beings are basically good and that beneath the surface of each of us, there exists something good. Based on his thought, he usually looks for something good in each person he meets. Sometimes the good is more obvious, but when he looks, he can always find the treasure, however deeply buried it is. Friends say that Mickey is nice, that he is easy to get along with. I see that Mickey has a thought about people and that his reality follows from his thought. He makes it easy for people to be nice to him by meeting them in a nonjudging way, expecting to find a jewel. Instead of a negative feedback loop, he creates a positive one.

The Bible says, "As a man thinketh, so shall he be." But how can we possibly take charge of our thoughts? Surely you don't wake up in the morning saying, "Today is a great day to be negative. I guess I'll assume that everyone is out to get me, and I'll do it to them before they do it to me."

When you can begin to be an observer of your thoughts, you are immediately less caught up in them. It's not that all the negativity stops, but you can undoubtedly begin to see it as less real. As you become more experienced in meditation, you are more able to establish yourself as the observer.

Meditation has given me a two-fold gift: In general, my thoughts are now more benevolent and less judgmental. When I do become aware that I am thinking negatively, I find it easier to let the thought go and to return to my more peaceful state.

Thoughts are mind noise, and meditation quiets the noise so that we can listen to our true inner wisdom. The Quakers call that inner wisdom "the still, small voice within us, the voice of our intuitive hearts."[1]

If in our daily lives we can smile, if we can be peaceful and happy, not only we, but everyone will profit from it.

—Thich Nhat Hanh,
Being Peace

Chapter Eleven
Illness and Healing

I have been and still am a seeker, but I have ceased to question stars and books; I have begun to listen to the teachings my blood whispers to me.

—Hermann Hesse,
Prologue to *Demian*

Illness and Healing

What is healing? Is it fixing? Freud would have said so. He believed that a person was "cured" when he could return to living his life in the same neurotic way he had before his problems forced him to seek help. He likely would have agreed with the bumper sticker that says, "Life is hard and then you die." This is simply not true.

It is a dangerous trap to believe that healing must be fixing or curing. When this happens, we feel that we are worthy only when we are "fixed."

Healing is something very different. I believe that a person is healed when she has grown towards a life of greater zest and enthusiasm...when she has become more of an individual...when she has found a meaning in her life...when she is happy to get up in the morning and pleasantly tired when she goes to bed at night. I believe that people are healed when they have nurtured and cultivated their own uniqueness...when they have begun to mine the vast supply of jewels that lives inside their hearts and souls. I believe a human being is healed when he has discovered a reason to live.

The great philosopher Nietzsche said, "He who has a why

can bear with any how."

In *Man's Search for Meaning*, Viktor Frankl observed that those people who survived the ravages of typhus in the German death camps were able to use their suffering as a vehicle to change and to grow. Even in the face of almost everything being taken away, the survivors held on to one last freedom—the freedom to choose one's attitude in any given circumstance. He saw that the people who lived were able to find meaning and purpose in their lives, in their own ways. Dr. Frankl believes that the essence of being human lies in searching for meaning and purpose. He says that we can discover this meaning and value through our actions and deeds, by finding value in love or in achievements at work, and by using suffering as a turning point—an opportunity to change in positive ways.

I have seen this same phenomenon hold true for people facing illness. In case after case I have seen that those who survive have used their illness and suffering as an opportunity to find new meaning in their lives and to become even better versions of the people they were before they became ill. It is to such a degree that people are able to change and to grow that I have heard, from not a few people, that in an odd way they are grateful for having become so ill.

Lawrence LeShan is known as the father of mind/body therapy and is the author of more than a dozen books, including *Cancer as a Turning Point* and *How to Meditate*. He strongly believes that there are certain psychological steps that people can take to increase their self-healing abilities. Those steps are directed at goals much like the ones described by Viktor Frankl. Dr. LeShan holds that each of us is different, and when we find our own unique song to sing, our own personal meaning, and our own rhythm in life, we can uncover the inner and outer conditions under which we can best heal.

In all of us there is a natural inclination to move toward healing and wholeness. When we begin to explore and to look for what is right in us, we encourage that inclination. It is essential that we move in the direction of this natural tendency—toward full engagement with life—whether this be a life of twenty weeks or twenty years.

Illness creates an opportunity—a demand—to move in this direction towards wholeness. Illness awakens in us, like a giant, monstrous wake-up call, the opportunity to become a seeker—to embark on a journey of self-exploration and to let go of aspects of ourselves that inhibit us from living fully and openly.

I regard illness as a turning point—a transformative opportunity to make changes. It is as if illness can be the searchlight that can light the darkness of the tunnel so that we may see through the tunnel and beyond the darkness to the light at the other side.

Nietzsche said, "That which does not kill me makes me stronger."

Angie was 29 years old when she discovered a lump in her breast. Her physician assured her that she was entirely too young to have breast cancer and suggested that she stop worrying. By the time Angie's cancer was finally diagnosed, it had spread to her lymph nodes.

This lovely young woman had a mastectomy and went

through almost a year of very difficult chemotherapy. During her medical treatment she hired a photographer to chronicle her journey in photographs, so that she would not forget where she had been. I met Angie after she had completed her chemotherapy, when she began to attend classes that I teach in meditation and imagery. Angie began a daily practice of meditation and weekly psychotherapy so that she could learn how to be more peaceful and to live in a way that gave her more satisfaction and had more meaning for her. Angie had been in therapy and had been meditating for several months when she began to wonder if her story, and the photographs that she had of herself, might be helpful to other women facing cancer.

Angie is 32 years old now. She has been free of cancer for three years. Her photographs are on display around the country. She has been featured in countless stories, and her picture has graced the covers of magazines. She told me recently that she is grateful for having had cancer because it has given her the opportunity to make a difference and to touch other people's lives. She says that she now, for the first time in her life, has a reason to live.

When we discover ways to do this—to begin to live more fully—and we begin to move in this direction, several things begin to happen:

1. Our lives get better.

2. We begin to notice more of life around and within us (we become more mindful).

3. We begin to give a message to our bodies—to our immune systems—that we care, and we are worth saving.

There is very solid data which indicates that we very

probably can influence our healing and impact the way in which our bodies function. We can safely say that certain kinds of psychological action can affect immune system response.

A ten-year study done by Drs. Spiegel, Kraemer, Bloom, and Gottheil at Stanford University clearly indicated that women with metastatic breast cancer who participated in supportive group therapy, which included instructions on relaxation and self-hypnosis, lived twice as long as identically diagnosed women who did not participate in the group.[1]

Another important study was conducted by Drs. Fawzi and Kemeny that looked specifically at immune system function in eighty patients diagnosed with malignant melanoma, who participated in a six-week psychiatric intervention that included instructions on the relaxation methods that I am describing in this book.

The results of that study were remarkable. The investigators found that, indeed, there were positive changes in the immune system functions of the participating patients. Specifically, there seemed to be an increase in the production of natural killer cells, which are integral in preventing the spread of cancer.[2]

Where is the healer within us, and how do we find it? These are questions that I am constantly asked. I know that beneath the level of consciousness there is in each of us a part that is trying to grow and to move in the direction of healing and wholeness.

Consciousness is dense. It is filled with all of our programs and tapes and ideas that we have created during our lives in an attempt to keep us safe. Consciousness is filled with all our mind chatter that keeps us so very busy analyzing and criticizing ourselves and others. Consciousness is often congested with worry, shame, and guilt, that block the doorway to living fully and richly.

Meditation can be the decongestant that opens the way to our inner healer—to the part of us that creates an opportunity for us to do more of what feels good to us and to live more fully in each moment.

I am certain that the best possibility for living longer lies in living better.

Chapter Twelve

Imagery

The imagination is the sun in the soul of man.

—Paracelsus

Imagery

Imagery is a placebo. There is nothing real about imagining a bright yellow lemon in front of you—and then imagining cutting a wedge out of that lemon and taking a big juicy bite out of that lemon. There is nothing real about that bite of lemon, yet my hunch is, if you participated in this experiment, you felt your mouth fill with saliva.

I love working with people—individually and in small groups, up to about twenty-five persons. I do not like public speaking. I have stage fright, and I have been known to experience a terribly upset stomach prior to standing up in front of an audience. I am asked to do quite a bit of public speaking, and I used to cringe at each invitation. I began to use imagery to rehearse my performances, and it made a remarkable difference. I would imagine being in front of an audience (it feels safe because I know it is not real), and I would imagine the audience looking very interested and smiling. I would see myself as very composed and prepared. In fact, I would see myself as absolutely charming. Again, it feels quite safe when it's not real. Finally, I would see the audience clapping and cheering when I completed my talk.

Each time that I use this tool to prepare, my seminars seem to go smoothly, and I even enjoy the presentation. What the mind sees the body believes, and for our purposes, imagery can be the symbol of the healing process.

Several years ago, I attended a conference on hypnosis that was held in San Francisco. The conference was in December, and the weather was blustery and chilly for someone accustomed to warm Florida sun. I had anticipated swimming for exercise in the hotel's indoor lap pool, but I discovered that the pool was closed for repair. There was an outdoor pool, but the outdoor temperature was in the 50s–way out of my range of acceptability.

I had been recovering from a leg injury and had not run for several months, but discovering that this was one of my only options, I decided to try jogging. The health club at the hotel was equipped with a treadmill similar to the one that I had used before, and I started with a very slow jog.

I started and stopped soon afterwards because after five minutes I was winded and too exhausted to continue. Disappointed, I returned to my room and prepared for the day's workshops.

That afternoon, I attended a workshop on using visualization to improve performance. The workshop leader, a psychiatrist from Sweden, explained that he taught visualization techniques to train the Swedish tennis team that had been consistently winning the Davis Cup.

That evening, after my regular meditation, I spent about ten minutes visualizing myself running on the treadmill. In my mind's eye, I saw that run in as much detail as I could imagine.

I saw the time passing on the clock, I saw myself on the treadmill running at a particular speed. On my mental picture screen I watched the entire run, and saw myself completing forty minutes of jogging with no problems.

The next morning, with some trepidation, I began jogging on the treadmill. Directly in front of me was a picture window with a view of the city stretching before my eyes. It was dark outside when I started my run, but soon the dawn appeared and I was given the opportunity of watching the city shift from darkness and come alive with the early morning light. The process was so enchanting to me that I hardly noticed that I had been jogging for forty-five minutes!

Everything that we create begins in the mind. Creative works of art all begin with a picture, an image, a feeling, a melody, or a thought. The use of visualization has long been a technique that has been effective in training athletes. The Swedes and the Soviets have for years used visualization techniques to train their Olympic athletes. More recently, Americans have begun using imagery in training our competitive athletes.

Athletics is certainly not the only area where the use of imagery and creative visualization can be effective tools. Whenever you think of something, you are using imagination. Think of taking a soft piece of velvet and running it over the back of your hand. Can you feel the softness?

I am usually quite hungry by the end of my work day. It is frequently past 8 P.M. and I may not have eaten for several hours. There is a popular barbecued chicken restaurant that I pass on my way home each evening. The aroma that wafts through my car as I pass the restaurant calls up instant images of tasty chicken and ribs, and my mouth waters instantly. Perhaps you can recall such an experience.

What the mind sees, the body believes. It is easy to fool the mind and the body. They cannot tell the difference between what is real and what is imagined. This ease in trickery can be a double-edged sword, for it is equally simple to creatively imagine negative dreams and illusions. How long might it take for my mind to believe that I am incompetent if I continually tell myself that? It wouldn't take too long to convince yourself of any imagined quality or state of mind. In most healing traditions, imagery and visualization are used for positive purposes. One can envision being loving, peaceful, forgiving, and generous. It is possible to imagine vividly how it would be to feel more secure and serene or to have more energy. The possibilities are endless, and guided imagery audio tapes such as mine or countless others are more popular than ever. I have seen them for sale in book and record stores, in grocery stores, and even in convenience food marts at gas stations.

Imagery and Disease

For most people, a diagnosis of a grave disease is in the realm of the unthinkable and is associated with extreme feelings of despair, anxiety, anger, and stress. There are so many terrors that seem to immediately follow a determination of profound illness: fear of pain, disfigurement, abandonment, and death.

It is clear that the mind and the body are intimately linked and that one interacts with and affects the other. If one is in chaos, the other is affected and reacts. If you are not feeling well, the world looks gray and bleak. If the world and, in particular, your life, look dismal, it is not unlikely that you may soon feel the effects of a virus, headache, backache, or more serious illness. Just as physiology affects mood, feeling influences the body and all of its systems. Fear, anxiety, and stress act as immunosuppressants, stifling the production of natural killer cells and normal antibodies that we need to ward off disease.

Throughout human history, there have been those who wanted to be the best possible beings that they could, and they wanted to feel as well as they conceivably could. All across the land, people have invented practices for effecting this. Though the details differed depending on culture and socialization, the basic exercises are quite similar, and are called meditation. Imagery, the synthesis of hypnosis and meditation, has proven to be a consequential agent of change.

The imagery process is like planting a seed, and when that seed grows on the inside it bears fruit. Imagery creates a new belief system for the body, and when you work on this each day, much like you would nurture a garden, remarkable changes can happen. These tools, imagery and meditation, can have a dramatic influence in reducing pain, anxiety, and fear, and in fighting disease.

Imagery is thoughts that use the senses: hearing, seeing, tasting, touching, smelling. It can be a powerful component of much healing work, since however you think about yourself in a given situation, or at a given time, is going to determine what chemicals are released in your body. If you believe that life is filled with wonder, meaning, and challenge, you will feel hopeful. And if you believe that you are about to be hit over the head with a club, you are going to feel afraid. In both cases, your body will be the recipient of the chemicals associated with your feelings. It seems that the inner creates the outer and the invisible creates the visible. As you begin to heal, you will see differently and your body will produce different, more healing chemicals.

It would be wonderful if we were able to simply tell our bodies to do exactly what we want. In some respects we can: we can decide to wiggle our toes or blink our eyes. We are not able to tell our salivary glands to produce more saliva, but imagining that juicy lemon can produce the effect. We can't tell our hearts to slow down, but imagine resting comfortably under an umbrella, on a vast beach of white glistening sand, with the sun shining brightly and a gentle breeze keeping you cool. Imagine the feeling of the sun and the breeze as you rest, untroubled and at peace. I believe that your heart rate may begin to change as you feel yourself more and more a part of the picture in your mind.

You may not be able to consciously will something to change in your body, but you can imagine it vividly enough to create the possibility of it becoming real.

There is a well-known true story about a man diagnosed with cancer. At the time of his diagnosis there was a new drug on the market that was said to be effective in his type of cancer. The drug was Krebiozen, and the man was given the drug and was told that the drug would certainly cure him.

Within a short time he was, indeed, cured, and his cancer

disappeared. He went out and lived his life and was happy.

Shortly thereafter a report came to light that indicated that Krebiozen was not really the miracle cure that it had been advertised as. Within weeks the man was sick and he returned to his doctor, only to be told that his cancer had recurred. The physician was, by that time, certain that Krebiozen was worthless, but having no other therapy to offer the man, he lied and said that although the media had hinted at the ineffectiveness of the drug, he was a doctor and he knew the real story. He told the man that Krebiozen was, indeed, the miracle drug that they had believed it to be, and once again, the physician assured the man that the drug would save him. The man agreed and was given a dose of what he believed to be Krebiozen. In fact, it was only a saline solution. Salt water!

Just as before, the cancer disappeared, and the man was able to enjoy his life—until about six months later, when the final reports on the drug were released to the media, and it was reported that Krebiozen was completely worthless. The man died within two weeks of reading the report.

The common denominator of the experiment with imagining a bite into a wedge of lemon and the man who was cured with Krebiozen is expectation. If we believe and expect that something may happen, it is likely that it can.

There is no "right" way to use imagery—only your way. Some people prefer to use audio tapes. If you choose to use a tape, this is fine, so long as you do not replace your regular practice of meditation with a tape. The two practices are quite different and though they can be done concurrently, one ought not replace the other.

If you should choose to create your own healing image, know that we all have different ways to imagine. Only about 60 percent of people use visual imagery. You must be able to find your own way to imagine. You may feel things, or sense things, or even smell things. Perhaps you can imagine hearing or tasting more easily.

Jeanne had breast cancer. She was anxious to include imagery as a part of her whole healing program which included the best of modern medicine, the best of psychotherapy, and the best of her own inner healing resources. She told me that it was difficult for her to see pictures in her mind. She loved classical music, and I asked her if she could hear her favorite musical piece in her head. That was easy for her, so she began to create a healing sound. She wanted the sound to be one that would destroy any cancer cells that might have remained in her body. Perhaps you have heard the sound a bug makes as it hits the light on a bug lamp. That is the sound that Jeanne heard, and she imagined that each *zap* was a cancer cell being destroyed. It might not have been the sound that I would have used, but this felt right for her. That is crucial in this work. You must find an image that feels right for you.

Herm is a cancer survivor. He has been free of illness for many years, but each week he enlists the help of an imaginary army of mean-looking little creatures to patrol his entire body and destroy any abnormal cells. He imagines this army of warriors traveling through his body on a search and destroy mission.

Many people prefer to create, in their mind's eye, an image that accurately represents the way in which the immune system actually battles and conquers the invaders that find their way into our bodies. Libraries are an excellent resource for material, stocked with both books and video tapes that illustrate this process.

There is some debate comparing the benefits of "hard" and "soft" images in fighting illness. Herm's image is hard. He gets in there with his team and destroys whatever doesn't look right. A soft image might be a gentle brook softly washing away any diseased cells. Many professionals feel that a "hard" image is better, that disease is no friend to be treated with respect and kindness. Others say that it is important to love all the parts of you and that even disease is a part of you.

I believe that it does not matter if your image is hard or soft so long as you have some belief in the possibility that it might help. That is all that matters: your belief in the possibility that your own healing symbol can be your ally in the fight for your life.

Imagery is a gift. Like meditation, imagery is a pathway that can lead to the jewel inside of us—to our own self-healing resources. All inner gifts must be taken seriously if they are to be effective, and imagery is no exception.

It is important to use imagery at least twice a day when you are actively fighting illness. Later on, after you are recovered, or of you are using imagery for other purposes, it's fine to do it only when you feel the need.

Patients can actively work to visualize parts of the body that may be involved with the disease, and then see the healing agent somehow destroy the diseased parts. Some of the images that people use are very creative. Sue, a cancer patient, imagined that tiny, powerful explosives were being discharged in strategic spots in her body and were blasting away the cancer cells. Greg imagined using a pail and shovel, like a child uses at the beach, to dig out the disease from his body.

I believe that we ought to approach with caution. Guided imagery and meditation are not identical, and the differences are quite significant. The practice of meditation teaches us how to be in our world. There is no goal, only to have an awareness of the moment...to be mindful. Though it is certainly often true that peace of mind, improved health, and self-esteem follow from meditation, these are not the goals...only the gifts. Guided imagery and visualization are goal-directed and very specific.

Sometimes, it is sufficient to simply practice meditation regularly and let your body heal and take care of itself. Frequently, that may not be enough, and if you care to use imagery and visualization, do so as an adjunct to meditation, not in place of your daily ritual. I encourage people to spend a few extra minutes at the end of their regular meditation to use guided imagery. Meditation can empty the mind of old worn-out, useless pictures and thoughts, and thus create the space for a new way of being. Visualizing what we want to be, or how we see our paths unfolding, can be what our minds create. Always remember that what you see can be what you get.

Guided imagery is not a panacea. Sometimes it works in reducing or even eliminating disease. It would be unethical and inaccurate for me to state that these tools can always cure. Perhaps the most valuable offering that imagery and meditation can give to all people, ill and well, is the gift of hope. If we can hope to live each day fully, one day at a time, there is no limit to the magic we can create.

Imagination is more important than knowledge.

—Albert Einstein

Chapter Thirteen
Exercise and Healing

The meaning of Life can be found only in the experience of living.

—Noah benShea,
Jacob's Journey

Exercise and Healing

There is a wonderful Hasidic tale about a rabbi who was going to visit a small village in Russia. The townspeople were looking forward to the visit, and each thought long and hard about what questions they might ask the wise man. They gathered in a large meeting hall, armed with their questions, and awaited his arrival. The rabbi came into the room and immediately felt the great tension in it. At first he said nothing and then he began to softly hum a Hasidic melody. Soon, all the villagers were humming the tune along with him.

Shortly, he began to dance, and the townspeople joined him, caught up in the movement. Within a few moments they were all intimately involved in the dance, unaware of all else, save for the movement of their bodies and the rhythm of the music. They danced. That was all they did, and in dancing, they got in touch with a part of themselves—the place where understanding and learning exist. Soon, the rabbi slowed down the dance, finally coming to rest. He looked at the group and said, "I trust that I have answered all your questions."[1]

Mindfulness is one of the greatest gifts we can ever hope

to receive. Like meditation, exercise prompts us to learn to do one thing at a time: to learn mindfulness. Though in many ways the two endeavors are very different, in some important ways they are quite similar and enhance the effects of each other.

The most obvious difference is movement. Most meditation is still, the only movement being quiet, rhythmic breathing. A meditator sits peacefully, focusing on breathing or silently repeating a mantra. Breathing is deep, metabolism slows down, as do the pulse and heart rate. Unless one is meditating in the hot sun or in a room with diminished airflow, it is unlikely that there will be a lot of perspiration during the meditation. The relaxation response is elicited by repetition.

Meditation helps us to become stronger inside: to become less suspicious, less vulnerable, with the corollary being a less hostile person, one who is easier to be with. Meditation can fine tune a person so that he can more easily move towards his goal.

Physiologically, as I discussed earlier, meditation has a dramatic effect on the body. The relaxation response has been clearly shown to enhance the immune system, and meditators are often less troubled by illness and can frequently have some effect on the course of their ills. Meditators are frequently able to sleep better, and may be more efficient during their waking hours.

It is widely acknowledged that meditation is a key in reducing the damaging effects of stress. Not only can it help in this way, but it may change your entire perception of stress. Things that habitually bothered me before I began meditating rarely get to me now. When they do, the effects do not last for long, and my natural peace of mind soon returns.

I might easily have used exercise in place of meditation in most of the examples of the positive effects of meditation. For instance, when I complete a run, I feel terrific. Though wet with perspiration, I feel strong, positive, and in control; I feel competent and powerful. I feel less vulnerable and less wary, and I know that I am easier to be with. This sounds remarkably similar to the effects of meditation.

Both disciplines train and fine tune a person, making it easier to move towards goals. Both involve the rhythmic repetition of a particular movement, and both can induce the relaxation response. When this happens, the left and the right brain act more in harmony, and the conscious and unconscious seem to work together, leading to an increased openness to change.

Like meditation, exercise helps to create optimism. More and more importance is being given to the physiological consequences of optimism. Self-hatred and denial are excellent predictors of disease, and these traits can be healed and changed through a sense of control that comes as a by-product of exercise. There is a fine sense of competence and accomplishment that goes along with finishing a four-mile run, a three- or four-mile walk, one-half hour on a Stairmaster, or thirty minutes of any constant aerobic activity that gets your heart pumping.

If you are a regular exerciser, you've probably experienced the wonderful feelings of "runner's high." It is believed that these feelings are caused by neurotransmitters called endorphins. Endorphins are natural opiates produced by the body, and there is more and more evidence that they aid the activity of the immune system in much the same way that meditation does.

Just as too much meditating (more than twenty minutes at a time) seems to have a negative effect on the mind, too much exercise can be damaging as well. Though exercise is something positive that we can give to ourselves, too much of this good thing can be damaging. I have to be careful not to become addicted to my endorphin high. I love the feeling I get from running, and if my body could take it, I might be tempted to run several miles every day. I have known runners who have become so addicted to the sport that they have neglected their families and businesses. I have witnessed marriages and businesses fail because not enough attention was given to them. Anything can be addictive, especially if the "anything" makes us feel good, if it is legal, and if it is seen as something positive.

Physiologically, too much exercise can be damaging to the body. While moderate exercise seems to boost the immune system, there is mounting evidence that too much exercise suppresses immune function. Thomas Tomasi, M.D., Ph.D., an immunologist who heads the Roswell Park Cancer Institute in Buffalo, conducted several studies that support this hypothesis. He studied nationally ranked Nordic skiers and competitive bicyclists and found, "…when you are in a severe competition such as the national ski races, or when you push people in the laboratory to the wall—where there is maximum exertion over a prolonged period—that harms certain aspects of the immune response."[2] Researchers studying runners in the

1987 Los Angeles Marathon concluded, similarly, that "over-doing" exercise can cause higher rates of infectious illness.

"Everything in moderation." This is a phrase that I have heard for such a long time. The real essence of it evaded me until now. Have you ever wondered how flamingos and storks are able to stand on one leg for long periods of time, without falling on their faces? I have been intrigued for years, perhaps because strength and balance were unfamiliar to me for so long. I believe that they have very strong legs and a remark-able sense of balance. It is my belief that exercise and meditation can help us to attain these gifts: stronger bodies and minds, more resilience, and more physical and emotional balance in life. I know that the discipline necessary is a small price to ask when the rewards can be so exquisite.

Chapter Fourteen
Conscious Eating

In the land of the spirit, you cannot walk by the light of someone else's lamp. You want to borrow mine. I'd rather teach you how to make your own.

—Anthony deMello,
One Minute Wisdom

Conscious Eating

I do not believe that we can be truly mindful and live each day to the fullest without paying some attention to what we put into our bodies. Just as we hope to be more aware of what is going on in our minds, and to be more in control of what we pay attention to, so we need to pay better attention to and be more in control of the food that we use to nourish ourselves.

Though science and medicine have allowed us to, probably, be healthier than ever before, there is mounting evidence that our health is being damaged by overeating and by eating certain harmful foods and chemicals.

We are eating things that the human body never imagined before. Artificial food is everywhere. Imitation butter, fish, eggs, cheese, fat, and sugar are the hottest-selling items in many grocery stores. This is not to say that these products are bad, but that we must be aware that we truly do not know the long term effects of these chemicals on our bodies.

I am certainly not a purist. In fact, I am quick to try new food products. I liberally sprinkle bogus butter on my baked potatoes, make delicious omelets with no eggs, and sweeten my tea with sugary-tasting artificial ingredients. I am not advocating a totally pure diet—this must be your decision—but we need to be aware of the potential for problems.

I doubt that anyone could argue against the idea that diet is a major influence in heart disease. Americans eat more fat than people in almost any other country. The cheese, bacon, butter, beef, and creamy foods that we eat so much of are very proficient at clogging the arteries. This, in turn, can lead to heart disease.

High levels of fat in the diet are implicated in many types of cancer. Much research has shown that many people diagnosed with breast and colon cancer ate diets significantly higher in fat than what is considered reasonable.

But how do we become more aware of our diet, and even more importantly, how do we change what we eat? It appears that strict diets do not work. They may be effective over the short term, and occasionally someone who takes off a lot of weight by dieting can maintain the weight loss. But far more frequently, all the weight is regained. In fact, the "yo-yo syndrome" of weight control (in which weight is continually lost and regained) appears to have an effect on the metabolism. It appears that this up and down pattern can significantly slow the metabolism, thus making it more difficult, each time, to lose weight.

As we have seen, meditation can be extremely useful in becoming aware of and changing patterns of thought and behavior. We can make positive changes in our lives and become more efficient and certainly happier. Our connection with food is no different. As we grow more mindful and aware, we can naturally develop more esteem for ourselves and will want to treat our bodies with more love and respect.

In a place of mindfulness, I believe we are able to know what foods are healing for us. I have a rather simple test that I use. After I eat something, I check to see how I feel, inside my body. If I feel energized, alive and well, I believe the food is good for me. On the other hand, if I feel weighed down, heavy, and tired, or if I feel "buzzed" and speedy, I know that what I have eaten is not right for me.

Janet was not obese, though she was in a constant battle with twenty pounds. She was referred to me when her doctor diagnosed her hypertension. She reported that her job was very stressful, and she often went to the candy machine as a way of taking a break and relaxing at work. In fact, she said that she often ate as a way of calming her nerves, whether she was hungry or not. A part of Janet's therapy was to begin a daily practice of mindfulness meditation.

After two months of meditating, Janet had lost fifteen pounds. This had not been the reason she came to see me. Her hypertension was also relieved, and her blood pressure returned to normal. Finding a calm place inside of her, an internal peace, was more satisfying to her and met her needs even more that the candy had.

I am not championing any particular food plan, and I do not suggest that you eat more or less of any specific food. I only propose that we can be more mindful about all the activities of daily living. Thoughts drift through our minds like leaves falling from a tree, and we are no longer compelled to scrutinize each one. So it can be with food. The choices are ours.

Chapter Fifteen

Shopping for New Glasses— Reframing What You See

Inside yourself or outside, you never have to change what you see, only the way you see it.

—Thaddeus Golas,
The Lazy Man's Guide to Enlightenment

Shopping for New Glasses— Reframing What You See

The way we see life is determined by the frame of reference, or the glasses, that we happen to be using to view the world at a particular moment in time. Frames of reference, like moods, are not constant. In fact, frames of reference are often dependent on mood. Have you noticed that when you are in a good mood, you are likely to be far more tolerant of others, even more liberal and open-minded in your views, more willing to listen to someone else and to take a look through their glasses?

Relationships frequently suffer from the effects of changing frames of reference. All too often, the qualities that we found engaging and endearing in our partner during the courtship stage, when moods are positive and pleasant, become the sources of annoyance and displeasure when the honeymoon is over.

When couples come to counseling for help, I ask each of them what they see as the problem. Frequently, each of them will have a laundry list of complaints about the other. She is selfish, he is stingy, he is sarcastic, she is a snob, etc. I also ask each of them for the qualities that attracted them to the other. The answers are amusing. She was independent and could really take care of herself, he was so good at managing his money, he had a terrific, dry sense of humor, and she seemed to choose such interesting people to be around.

Nothing has really changed except for their attitudes and the glasses that they now see each other through. When you change your attitude, everything changes.

Our attention is usually focused on finding evidence to support our beliefs, and our beliefs are often colored by our moods. It's as if your moods are the filters through which your beliefs are created, and your beliefs are the filters through which, on a moment-to-moment basis, you are created.

In many ways it is true that you are what you see, and you see through the filters of who you are at that moment. Scientists agree that what you see in front of you is neither a complete picture of what is there, nor is it a completely true picture.

Eknath Easwaran gives an example of this when he describes four people walking down Main Street. Ask each of them what they notice, and the answers are interesting.

The businessman, just returning from a business lunch, notices the large crowd at Delfini's Department Store and comments on the marketing ability of their management.

An elderly schoolteacher remarks that it is nice to see Mr. Delfini's son, George, working in the family business.

A teenage girl notices the great sale on shoes, and the teenage boy notices the girls shopping for the shoes.[1]

Each description is a product of the individual's frame of reference as seen through that person's unique set of glasses. Perhaps at another time, these same four people would see quite differently.

Unfortunately, it is often the case that we have little control over what we see. It's as if our minds project a story on the screen of our awareness, and we are compelled to watch it. But how about the film that is showing? Do we have some control over the viewing and choice of film? If we are to find some peace and freedom in our lives, we must learn that we are not always at the mercy of our thoughts and attention. We can develop some self-determined control over what we see and over what we choose to pay attention to.

Meditation can help you to gain that degree of control over what you think and what you see. When this miracle happens, the whole world will look very different to you. More and more you will be able to see through the filters of your mood to what truly is—to the essence of things. When you can cut through the filters, you can begin to see with more clarity. How lovely to be able to see the connection of all things living—to see the order of life. With the practice of meditation, you can look for the treasures that life can afford, and not feel forced to look for the potholes.

A wonderful benefit, for me, has been the ability to have some distance from what I see—to see with more perspective. Often, when I can stand back from what I perceive, I can see the bigger picture, and it is frequently rather funny.

Historically, if anyone mimicked me, it would make me furious. It was a real button-pusher. It's not too startling that I would have this kind of reaction to mimicking, as I can remember my mom becoming infuriated with my dad any time he mimicked her.

A few weeks ago, my husband and I were having a

peaceful evening together. I was reading and Herm was watching television. I got up from my chair to get something, and Herm asked me to switch the channel for him. As soon as I put on the channel that I thought was the correct one, I heard him say, in a voice that was clearly intended to sound like mine, "Teriiiiiiiiiiii, you put the wrong channel onnnnnnnnnnnnnnn."

My first reaction was to want to scream at him, "Don't ever mimic me!" But instead, I listened to the sound I heard, the sound he must hear when I whine, and it struck me so funny that I started to laugh. I knew I would not ever whine like that again.

It is only with perspective that we can hope to see anything new and to learn from what we see. With new eyes and new ears, we can see the newness and freshness of everything.

The dust and stones of the street were as precious as gold...The green trees...transported and ravished me; their sweetness and unusual beauty made my heart to leap...Boys and girls tumbling in the street...were moving jewels...Eternity was manifested in the light of the day, and something infinite behind everything appeared.

—Thomas Traherne

Chapter Sixteen
A Change of Mind

That day I saw beneath dark clouds the passing light over the water and heard the voice of the world speak out. I knew then, as I had before, life is no passing memory of what has been nor the remaining pages in a great book waiting to be read.

It is the opening of eyes long closed. It is the vision of far off things seen for the silence they hold. It is the heart after years of secret conversing speaking out loud in the clear air. It is Moses in the desert fallen to his knees before the lit bush. It is the man throwing away his shoes as if to enter heaven and finding himself astonished, opened at last, fallen in love with solid ground.

—David Whyte,
Songs for Coming Home

A Change of Mind

I n 1962, Thomas Kuhn introduced the term "paradigm shift." Though his focus was science, the term has come to encompass all dramatically new ways of thinking. We speak of paradigm shifts in medicine, architecture, education, and so on.

In 1980, Marilyn Ferguson, in her inspirational book *The Aquarian Conspiracy*, wrote that we have entered into a paradigm shift in consciousness.[1]

Like all paradigm shifts, this one comes following a time of crisis. The first fifty years of this century were fraught with terror, war, breakdown, and undoing.

Though the war in Vietnam continued into the 1960s, that same decade marked the beginning of exploration in other directions as well. We began the exploration of outer space, and we began investigating our inner space. The seeds of looking for peace in the proper places had been planted and were beginning to germinate.

Edgar Mitchell, one of the original Apollo 14 astronauts, had a vision from the moon. He saw Earth as a living organism that needed protection from the corruption of humankind. He saw that we could destroy our land and ourselves, by war on each other and by war on our land. He believed that we must dedicate ourselves to peace, not to power.

In 1973, several years after his historic voyage to the moon, Edgar Mitchell founded The Institute of Noetic Sciences to support research and education on human consciousness. Today, his institute is one of many driving forces illustrating that the true paths to power are inside each of us.

A change of consciousness is occurring, and this is the only way to transform the world. I believe that the universe will change only as we bring into balance, within each of us, mind, body, and spirit.

In all corners, our assumptions about reality are being challenged. Our ideas about the physical and biological sciences are being questioned. We are wondering, more than ever, about the brain and about memory. Rupert Sheldrake and Larry Dossey have both speculated that, perhaps, the human mind is not confined to the brain—that the mind, perhaps, uses the brain as a conduit, much like electricity acts through a wire, but is not created by the wire. Perhaps, they speculate, there might be a consciousness that exists within another dimension.[2]

Scientists such as Candace Pert, formerly of the National Institute of Mental Health, wonder if there may be a form of communication that occurs between the cells in our bodies, independent of the brain. Roger Sperry and others have theorized that consciousness creates objects, depending on the density of the energy.

It is not only in the physical and biological sciences that we are beginning to notice a paradigm shift, but certainly in the human sciences, in the realm of the spirit, we are noticing dramatic changes in our assumptions.

"Psychics," "channelers," and "psychic awareness" are all buzzwords around the weekend seminar circuit. I hold that, indeed, psychic awareness is becoming more and more important, but that awareness is developing as we come to have a deeper trust for our own intuition, for our personal psychic awareness. More and more, we are concluding that the answers to all of our questions lie within our own consciousness. Perhaps, we are reclaiming what we once had, but lost somewhere along the way. I heard someone refer to meditation as "coming home." It is the process by which we tap into what is already established inside each of us—our inner wisdom. Whether it be to travel inside to find peace and balance or to seek the inspiration for a painting or a poem, the solutions come from us. No one can instill creativity, ethics, or integrity in us. We must find them ourselves.

Then, having touched the loving, creative qualities within ourselves, we can seek them in others. When we know that goodness exists within us, and that we are a part of all humankind, we will look for it in our sisters and brothers.

Since we always find whatever we look for, we will touch the good in others, and they can then become aware of it in themselves. And so the process of a paradigm shift in consciousness continues.[3]

Chapter Seventeen
Personal Trance

A tree that can fill the span of a man's arms grows from a
   downy tip;
A terrace nine stories high rises from hodfuls of earth;
A journey of a thousand miles starts from beneath one's
   feet.

—Lao-tzu

Personal Trance

We all live in a personal hypnotic trance. Our basic assumptions shape the reality that we see, and that reality becomes the trance in which we live each day. With the quiet healing that meditation can bring, we can change the trance that we live in. We can welcome the learnings and insights that emerge from inside ourselves. We can transform our inner vision and live in a changed world.

The Berlin Wall has tumbled down. Eastern Europe has begun to see the light of democracy. As the boundaries and politics between and in nations have changed, creating a new world view, so can the limits of what we personally know expand and change.

I believe that a new world is possible and that it begins with learning to trust ourselves.

Beneath the trappings of our beliefs lies a whole other world. If we truly seek peace, we must not look on the outside. Peace cannot be found in material goods that are state of the art, or in speeches about the state of the nation. Peace is a state of mind.

Václav Havel: (To his wife, Olga Havel, from prison)

We must constantly, here, now,
at once and everywhere,
withstand the temptation
to be utilitarian
and we must weigh what is true
against what is a lie,
what is genuine against what is false,
what is moral against what is immoral,
what is life-giving against what is deadening.

We must never forget
that the first little lie
told in the interest of truth,
the first little injustice
committed in the name of justice,
the first tiny immorality
defended by the morality of things,
the first careless lapse
in this constant vigilance
means the certain beginning of the end.
Hope is a dimension of the spirit.
It is not outside us but within us.
When you lose it you must seek it again
Within yourself
and with people around you
Not in objects
Or even events.

Epilogue

Healing Made Manifest

Come to the edge, he said.
They said: We are afraid.
Come to the edge, he said.
They came.
He pushed them...and they flew.
—Guillaume Apollinaire

Healing Made Manifest

I was quite young when my parents began sending me to summer camp. I am certain that it must have been a well-deserved opportunity for them to have time off from parenting, and it was equally as much a time of celebration for me. Although I was very young, I was able to notice differences in the way I felt and in the things I did while a part of the community of campers. It seemed to me that I was more energetic, that I stretched farther, and ran faster—that I was a better version of me. It was as if being in the company of others motivated me to do more and to *be* more than I had been. Today I know that the power of community can be a mighty force in healing.

In my work as a psychotherapist, many of the people who come to see me are facing life-threatening illness. As I began to work more and more with these people, I wondered if the power of community could be harnessed to potentiate the self-healing abilities of individuals. I believed that if children were able to borrow and use the inner strength of one another, certainly people facing cancer, AIDS, multiple sclerosis, and other life-threatening illnesses might do the same. I have already mentioned the groundbreaking studies done by Drs. Spiegel and Fawzi, which clearly showed this to be true in outpatient settings, but I believed that a residential setting might be even more powerful.

I wrote several proposals and presented them to the boards of directors of local hospitals and to oncologists in this community. In all cases I was met with enthusiasm and encouragement. However, the support stopped there. Not once was there any further mention of such a program. I knew that I was up against the powerful force of skepticism and even disbelief. I continued the work I was doing and knew that, one day, a program such as the one I dreamed of would come alive.

I am blessed with having as a colleague, a mentor, and a friend, Larry LeShan, known worldwide as the father of mind/body therapy. Several years ago we began to compare our hopes and dreams, and we recognized that, together, we might create such a healing community. We worked for a very long time planning a program that could very dramatically awaken people's self-healing resources in ways that could help them to respond better to medical treatment, to be more enthusiastic, to live better and even, possibly, live longer.

In October, 1993, The Institute for Mind-Body Health (formerly The Lawrence LeShan Institute), 1514 San Ignacio, Suite 150, Coral Gables, Florida 33146, telephone: 800-940-0584, began its first intensive, six-day residential program in the Florida Keys. Recently, we have begun to work in cooperation with The University of Miami School of Medicine and The Sylvester Comprehensive Cancer Center. The purpose of our program is to help people determine who they want to be, rather than who they should be.

Illness is an opportunity to make changes in one's life...to find more meaning...to find more enthusiasm...to find stronger and better reasons to live...and to find new ways of relating and creating that give one greater passion and spirit. The evidence supports the idea that living richly can have a positive effect on health and longevity. This and the incredible force of community support have combined to help make our program one that, from the anecdotal evidence, is having a dramatic effect on people's lives.

Our programs are small, and each session accommodates up to only twelve participants. We are open to anyone facing serious illness, and participants are often accompanied by a family member or other support person.

We have tried very hard to create a total healing environment. We've included intensive individual and group psychotherapy, training in meditation and imagery, exercise and therapeutic massage, nutritional counseling, art therapy—all provided by a staff of highly trained professionals who are steeped in the knowledge of science and the practice of spirit and love.

I believe that dreams can come true. Sometimes they change shape and form, and what we get may not look like what we asked for, but if we look beyond the form...to the essence...we can find the manifestation of our dreams.

When the mind is quiet and self-love comes calling, magic can happen.

I wish you well on your journey.

—Teri Amar

Notes

Over the years, I have collected a series of quotes that have touched me as reverberating with truth. I have used some of these quotes as epigraphs to introduce each chapter. Though in all cases I have noted the author of each quote, I have not always been able to locate the text that the quote originally appeared in. Whenever possible, the source has been indicated.

I've Been There, Too!

1. Borysenko, Joan. *Minding the Body, Mending the Mind.* New York: Bantam Books, 1987.

2. deMello, Anthony. *One Minute Wisdom.* New York: Doubleday Publishing Group, Inc., 1985.

Chapter 1

1. Dass, Ram. *Journey of Awakening: A Meditator's Guidebook.* New York: Bantam Books, 1978.

2. ———. *Be Here Now.* New York: Crown Publishing, 1971.

3. Rossi, Ernest Lawrence. *The Psychobiology of Mind-Body Healing*. New York: W.W. Norton & Co., 1986.

4. Benson, Herbert, and Miriam Z. Klipper. *The Relaxation Response*. New York: Avon Books, 1976.

Chapter 2

1. Benson, Herbert, and Miriam Z. Klipper. *Relaxation Response*.

2. LeShan, Lawrence. *Cancer as a Turning Point*. New York: Penguin Books, 1989.

3. Frankl, Viktor. *Man's Search for Meaning*. Boston: Beacon Press, 1963.

4. Rossi, Ernest Lawrence. *Psychobiology*.

5. Borysenko, Joan. *Minding the Body*.

Chapter 3

1. Borysenko, Joan. *Minding the Body*.

Chapter 4

1. Nelsen, Jane. *Understanding*. Rocklin, California: Prima Publishing, 1988.

Chapter 5

1.   Dass, Ram, and Paul Gorman. *How Can I Help?* New York: Alfred A. Knopf, Inc., 1988.

2.   LeShan, Lawrence. *How to Meditate*. New York: Bantam Books, 1974.

3.   Borysenko, Joan. *Minding the Body*.

Chapter 6

1. Hanh, Thich Nhat. *The Miracle of Mindfulness*. Boston: Beacon Press, 1975.

2. Borysenko, Joan. *Minding the Body*.

3. Dass, Ram. *Be Here Now*.

Chapter 7

1. Pelletier, Kenneth R. *Towards a Science of Consciousness*. New York: Delacorte Press, 1978.

2. ————. "Applications of Meditative Exercises in Enhancing Clinical Biofeedback Outcome," *Proceedings of the Biofeedback Research Society*. Denver: Biofeedback Research Society, 1976.

3. Kornfield, J. "Intensive Insight Meditation: A Phenominological Study," *Journal of Transpersonal Psychology*, 1979, 11 (1), 41-58.

Chapter 8

1. Dass, Ram, and Paul Gorman. *How Can I Help?*

2. LeShan, Lawrence. *How to Meditate*.

Chapter 10

1. Dass, Ram. *Journey of Awakening*.

Chapter 11

1. Speigel, D., and others. "Effects of Psychosocial Treatment on Survival of Patients with Metastatic Breast Cancer," *The Lancet*, 2, (1989): 888-891.

2. Fawzi, F.L., and others. "A Structured Psychiatric Intervention for Cancer Patients. II. Changes Over Time in Immunological Measures." *Archives of General Psychiatry,* 47, (1990): 927-935.

Chapter 13
1. LeShan, Lawrence. *How to Meditate.*
2. "Can You Walk Your Way to Maximum Immunity?" *Prevention Magazine.* April, 1990: 98.

Chapter 15
1. Easwaran, Eknath. *Meditation.* Petaluma: Nilgiri Press, 1978.

Chapter 16
1. Ferguson, Marilyn. *The Aquarian Conspiracy.* Los Angeles: J.B. Tarcher, Inc., 1980.
2. Dossey, Larry. *Recovering the Soul.* New York: Bantam Books, 1989.
3. Havel, Václav. "Signs of a World Awakening," *Noetic Sciences Review*, No. 14, Spring, 1990: 36.

Bibliography

If reading this book has stimulated your appetite for more knowledge, I offer you a bibliography of many of the books that I have learned from.

Meditation

Benson, Herbert, and Miriam Z. Klipper. *The Relaxation Response.* New York: Avon Books, 1976.

Benson, Herbert, and William Proctor. *Your Maximum Mind.* New York: Avon Books, 1987.

Borysenko, Joan. *Minding the Body, Mending the Mind.* New York: Bantam Books, 1988.

Dass, Ram. *Be Here Now.* New York: Crown Publishing, 1971.

———. *Journey of Awakening: A Meditator's Guidebook.* New York: Bantam Books, 1978.

Dass, Ram, and Stephen Levine. *Grist for the Mill.* Berkeley: Celestial Arts, 1976.

Easwaran, Eknath. *God Makes the Rivers to Flow.* Petaluma: Nilgiri Press, 1982.

————. *Meditation*. Petaluma: Nilgiri Press, 1987.

Fishel, Ruth. *The Journey Within*. Deerfield Beach: Health Communications, 1987.

Golas, Thaddeus. *The Lazy Man's Guide to Enlightenment*. Redway: Seed Center, 1972.

Hanh, Thich Nhat. *The Miracle of Mindfulness: A Manual of Meditation*. Boston: Beacon Press, 1976.

LeShan, Lawrence. *How to Meditate*. New York: Bantam Books, 1974.

Levine, Stephen. *A Gradual Awakening*. New York: Anchor Books, 1979.

Suzuki, Shunryu. *Zen Mind, Beginner's Mind*. New York: Weatherhill, 1970.

Healing and Medicine

Achterberg, Jeanne. *Imagery in Healing: Shamanism and Modern Medicine*. Boston: New Science Library, 1985.

Benson, Herbert. *The Mind/Body Effect*. New York: Simon & Schuster, 1979.

Cousins, Norman. *Anatomy of an Illness*. New York: W.W. Norton, 1979.

————. *The Healing Heart*. New York: W.W. Norton, 1983.

Dossey, Larry. *Space, Time and Medicine*. Boston: Shambhala, 1982.

————. *Recovering the Soul*. New York: Bantam Books, 1989.

LeShan, Lawrence. *Cancer as a Turning Point*. New York: Penguin Books, 1989.

Murphy, Michael, and Steven Donovan. *The Physical and Psychological Effects of Meditation*. Oakland: Dharma Enterprises, 1988.

Pelletier, Kenneth R. *Mind as Healer, Mind as Slayer*. New York: Dell Books, 1977.

Rossi, Ernest Lawrence. *The Psychobiology of Mind-Body Healing*. New York: W.W. Norton, 1986.

Siegel, Bernie. *Love, Medicine and Miracles*. New York: Harper and Row, 1986.

————. *Peace, Love and Healing*. New York: Harper and Row, 1989.

Psychology and Philosophy

Cheek, D., and L. LeCron. *Clinical Hypnotherapy*. New York: Grune and Stratton, 1968.

Dass, Ram, and Paul Gorman. *How Can I Help?* New York: Alfred A. Knopf, 1987.

deShazer, Steve. *Keys to Solutions in Brief Therapy*. New York: W.W. Norton, 1985.

Dostoevsky, Fyodor. *Notes from Underground*. New York: Dutton, 1960.

Erickson, Milton H. *The Collected Papers of Milton H. Erickson on Hypnosis*. New York: Irvington, 1980.

Ferguson, Marilyn. *The Aquarian Conspiracy*. Los Angeles: J.P. Tarcher, 1980.

Fields, Rick, and others. *Chop Wood, Carry Water: A Guide to Finding Spiritual Fulfillment in Everyday Life*. Los Angeles: Jeremy P. Tarcher, 1984.

Foundation for Inner Peace. *A Course in Miracles*. Farmingdale, New York: Foundation for Inner Peace, 1975.

Frankl, Viktor. *Man's Search for Meaning*. Boston: Beacon Press, 1963.

Gawain, Shakti. *Creative Visualization*. New York: Bantam Books, 1979.

Gawain, Shakti, with Laurel King. *Living in the Light*. San Rafael, California: New World Library, 1986.

Hudson-O'Hanlon, William, and Michele Weiner-Davis. *In Search Of Solutions*. New York: W.W. Norton, 1989.

May, Rollo. *Man's Search for Himself*. New York: Dell, 1953.

Nelsen, Jane. *Understanding*. Rocklin, California: Prima Publishing, 1986.

Peck, M. Scott. *The Road Less Traveled*. New York: Touchstone, 1978.

Peseschkian, Nossrat. *Oriental Stories as Tools in Psychotherapy*. New York: Springer-Verlag, 1979.

Sogyal Rinpoche. *The Tibetan Book of Living and Dying*. New York: HarperCollins Publishers, 1993.

Yalom, I. *Existential Psychotherapy*. New York: Basic Books, 1980.

Guided Imagery Audio Cassettes by Teri Amar, Ph.D.
Please send the following at $10.95 each:

	Quantity	Amount
City of Dreams by Teri Amar, Ph.D.	_____	$_____
Subtotal		_____
Fla. Res. add 6% tax		_____
Shipping & Handling		__$3.00
FedEx (add $15.50)		_____
Grand Total		$_____

Checks payable to Teri Amar, Ph.D.
Enclosed: $_____ (do not send cash)
or bill my [   ] VISA [   ] MasterCard

Card No._____Exp. Date_____

Signature_____

SHIP TO:

Name_____
Street_____
City_____State_____Zip_____
Phone (____)_____

Mail your order to:
    Teri Amar, Ph.D.
    1514 San Ignacio, Suite 150
    Coral Gables, FL 33146

If you would like information about THE INSTITUTE FOR
MIND-BODY HEALTH, please call (800) 940-0584.

About the Author

After studying journalism and English as an undergraduate at the University of Florida, Dr. Amar earned M.Ed. and Ph.D. degrees in psychology and has worked for many years in private practice providing psychological care and support to people facing life-threatening illnesses. She has been an adjunct assistant professor at the University of Miami Medical School. Dr. Amar has conducted meditation, imagery, and self-healing workshops, symposiums, and training programs throughout the United States. For several years, she has taught meditation and imagery and has been a facilitator for cancer support groups, offering her experience and support to families and caregivers.

"I try to act as a tour guide for people's journeys of self-exploration, and in so doing, help them become active participants in their lives and in their healing."

Dr. Amar is the founder and clinical director of The Institute for Mind-Body Health (formerly The Lawrence LeShan Institute), a residential treatment center in South Florida for people facing serious illnesses. The methods used at the Institute are designed to teach those with the illness and their families, friends, and other supporters how to use psychological change to help heal the patient's compromised immune system. Dr. Amar is now recognized as one of the leading U.S. practitioners in the growing field of mind-body therapy.